"Through powerful storytelling and bright images, Blair Imani sends a clear message to next-generation activists and changemakers—this is their moment, they are the present, the now, and yes, the future. Instead of waiting to be passed the proverbial torch, the heroes in Imani's book claim their role as torchbearers whose lights are blazing inspiring trails for each of us to follow."

—Jamia Wilson, executive director and publisher of Feminist Press

———

"I had chills while reading this entire book. THE ENTIRE BOOK. I was moved, inspired, and informed by the stories of these unbelievable people. I was also indignant: how could my history classes not have included such important pioneers?! Run out immediately and purchase multiple copies to send to your friends. I promise, they'll thank you."

—Claire Wasserman, CEO and founder of Ladies Get Paid

———

"Changing society's narrative often requires us to look back over our historical mosaic; admit what we got wrong; recognize who was silenced, marginalized, or erased; and then reorganize and rewrite. *Modern HERstory* offers an inclusive approach to this kind of truth-telling."

—Monica Lewinsky, anti-bullying advocate

MODERN HERSTORY

Foreword by
Tegan and Sara

Illustrations by
Monique Le

MODERN **HER**STORY

**Stories of Women and Nonbinary
People Rewriting History**

Blair Imani

TEN SPEED PRESS
California | New York

CONTENTS

Foreword by Tegan and Sara vi • Introduction viii

 LAYING THE GROUNDWORK 1

Sylvia Rivera & Marsha P. Johnson 5
Lorraine Hansberry 8
Patsy Takemoto Mink 11
Dorothy Vaughan, Mary Jackson & Katherine Johnson 12

2 LEADING THE MOVEMENT 17

Kimberlé Crenshaw 23
Alicia Garza 24
Patrisse Cullors 27
Opal Tometi 28
Carmen Perez 31
Linda Sarsour 32
Tamika D. Mallory 35

3 SPEAKING TRUTH TO POWER 37

Allison Renville 41
Brittany Packnett 42
Geraldine Roman 45
Jamilah Lemieux 46
Janet Mock 49
Keah Brown 50
Manal al-Sharif 53
Rokhaya Diallo 54
Dr. Roxane Gay 57
Sandy Ho 58

 THE REVOLUTION WILL BE LIVE 61

Ava DuVernay 65
Cameron Esposito 66
Constance Wu 69
Ellen DeGeneres 70
Leslie Jones 73
Missy Elliott 74
Oprah Winfrey 77
Serena Williams 78
Solange Knowles 81

5 MASTERING MODERN
MEDIA 83

Aditi Juneja 87
Amandla Stenberg 88
Feminista Jones 91
Franchesca Ramsey 92
Issa Rae 95
Jackie Aina 96
Kat Blaque 99
Michelle Phan 100
Mona Haydar 103
Taye Hansberry 104
Vilissa Thompson 107

6 THE REVOLUTION
WILL BE OURS 109

Dr. Adrienne Keene 113
Alencia Johnson 114
Anjali Paray 117
Jennicet Gutiérrez 118
Layshia Clarendon 121
Lori Rodriguez 122
Raquel Willis 125
Dr. Su'ad Abdul Khabeer 126
Winnie Harlow 129

7 THE REVOLUTION
WILL BE FUNDED 131

Amani Al-Khatahtbeh 135
Alissa Lentz 136
Eman Idil Bare 139
Ibtihaj Muhammad 140
Leslie Mac & Marissa Jenae Johnson 143
Rihanna 147
Shannon Coulter 148
Tegan & Sara 151

8 THE REVOLUTION IS NOW 153

Jazz Jennings 157
Mari Copeny 158
Marley Dias 161
Taylor Richardson 162
Yara Shahidi 165

Conclusion 166
Glossary
  Terms, Events,
  and Phrases 167
  People 173
  Organizations 180
  Hashtags 185

About the Author 187
About the Illustrator 188
Acknowledgments 190
Index 192

FOREWORD

Too often our society overlooks or undermines the value of young people and their contributions. Barely a week goes by without an op-ed investigating the lassitude of millennials or Xennials, and while this might be true of some, it is also worth noting that people of all ages can become disenfranchised, never investing time into bettering the world or themselves. So perhaps this is what is so noteworthy about Blair Imani and her tremendous contributions in such a brief period of time. Irrespective of age and experience, Blair has been instrumental in effecting change in multiple social and political movements in just a few short years. With this book adding to the dizzying list of gifts she's already given us, we declare Blair a radiant and dazzling example of hope and promise amidst the chaos.

One reason this book feels so moving and significant to us personally is because in 1987 our mother went back to school to get a bachelor's degree in social work. We were seven years old and our mother was in her late twenties—living on student loans and working part time while she educated herself to give us all a better life—when she had a **feminist** awakening. Soon her weekend afternoons (and ours by proxy) were spent at women's marches or hosting gatherings of like-minded women who were talking about the issues of the times. This was when, almost always exclusively in the company of women, we heard words like "herstory" and **"patriarchy"** for the first time. And it was at this moment that we had our own feminist awakening, the first of many. While nearly two decades have passed since we entered the adult world, we have cycled through different phases of political and social engagement. And as we've become more informed, we have become aware of how little we know of our herstory and its heroines. The significance of cross-generational awareness of our herstory is therefore important beyond measure.

We look to Blair as an example of how we should all approach this next chapter of herstory-telling and movement-making. To continue on the path that Blair lights for us, we must acknowledge those that have come before us and those currently confronting and challenging the status quo to enact change. We think *Modern HERstory* should be required reading for everyone, and we believe in our hearts that, with much darkness still to come, we have in Blair a brilliant luminary to guide us.

—TEGAN AND SARA

INTRODUCTION

When I was twelve years old, I realized that making a difference can be as simple as fighting for what you believe in, unapologetically living in your truth, or taking steps to improve the lives of others. I was fortunate to grow up with the constant encouragement from family and community members that I could realize the change I wanted to see in the world. Every one of us has the potential to make an indelible mark on our world; however, the stories of the ordinary heroes responsible for the most important social changes in history are often obscured. Studying history in college, I learned that it is usually written by those who have the most **privilege** and the most power. As a result, the contributions of diverse groups are often overlooked or erased, while those in power who uphold the status quo are praised as heroes.

Throughout history, diverse trailblazing individuals have been subjected to this erasure. For example, voting rights activist and civil rights leader **Fannie Lou Hamer** frequently goes unacknowledged in conversations about the **Civil Rights Movement**. Fannie Lou was a black woman born and raised in rural Mississippi, and she survived the violent oppressions faced by countless black women in the American South. After being fired from her job as a sharecropper simply because she registered to vote, she went on to dedicate her entire life to fighting for the rights of black people to direct their own futures. Fannie Lou was arrested and beaten for attempting to exercise rights, like voting, that America claims to promise to all its people. Similarly, few people are aware of the legacy of Chinese American experimental physicist **Chien-Shiung Wu**, a key contributor to the World War II–era American research initiative known as the Manhattan Project. The Nobel Prize for her award-winning and eponymous Wu Experiment was given to her male colleagues Tsung-Dao Lee and Chen-Ning Yang in 1957, despite the fact *she* developed it. Two **transgender** activists of color, **Sylvia Rivera** and **Marsha P. Johnson**, helped define the present state of **LGBTQ** rights organizing in the United States; however, their contributions continue to go unacknowledged within the LGBTQ community. Even a film documenting the historic event at which Sylvia and Marsha gained prominence, the 1969 Stonewall Riots, erased the presence of transgender women of color, instead centering the stories of white **gay cisgender** men.

While "history" focuses on men and the stories of patriarchs, *"herstory"* deliberately prioritizes the stories of women, people of color, and LGBTQ people. It was not until I reached adulthood that I began uncovering the truth about the many leaders and activists with whom I could relate. Realizing how important it is to understand and accurately represent herstory, I decided to become a walking encyclopedia of knowledge about diverse individuals who had made a difference in the past, as well as those making a difference in the present. I believe that the failure to acknowledge the heroic figures that have shaped our past should not hinder us from celebrating the individuals who are fighting to improve our present and future. In this book, I have gathered the stories of seventy such women and **nonbinary** individuals, which are accompanied by vibrant portraits created by artist **Monique Le**. The people featured in *Modern HERstory* come from different cultural backgrounds, abilities, sexual orientations, and **gender identities**, and have all contributed to activist movements and positive social change of recent history.

In this book, we will learn about individuals who combine innovative research from the academic arena with **grassroots** organizing strategies to drive progressive change. We will sing the praises of folks who make the world better by building community, living boldly in the face of oppression, and challenging the status quo. **Feminista Jones** makes life better for marginalized people in her community as a social worker, writer, and activist. **Jazz Jennings** makes history for transgender youth simply by living her life authentically in the face of blatant transphobia. **Manal al-Sharif** fought oppression through a simple act in defiance of her country's misogynistic laws. People like these show us that we all have the potential and the responsibility to make a difference, whether we become leaders of entire movements, educators who change lives, or community organizers who cultivate spaces for those pushed to the margins. Never in history has every demographic group been viewed as equal, nor has there been a moment in human history where oppression did not exist. Nevertheless, women, nonbinary folks, people of color, LGBTQ folks, people of faith, and disabled people have been fighting for a better future. It is time that we honor this truth and tell these stories. When we learn about the past and the state of the present, we can come closer to creating a world that values everyone's life. Today, many important grassroots organizers, educators, artists, and advocates are using their power to bring forward a more vibrant, equitable, and inclusive society.

Though I had an entire support system rooting for me from childhood and into my young adulthood, I still doubted myself and my ability to make a difference. For a long time, I carried the insecurity of my family being the only black family at my elementary school and the fear that I would be ostracized for my sexual orientation. Many of the individuals featured in *Modern HERstory* became the heroes and role models they needed growing up, just as I am trying to become the role model that I needed as a child. I hope that *Modern HERstory* can be a starting place for people of all ages, genders, abilities, and cultural origins to feel empowered in their potential to change the world for the better.

The power to influence government, improve communities, and create positive change is in our hands. With the right tools and the right knowledge, we can all be part of *Modern HERstory*.

CHAPTER
1

LAYING THE GROUNDWORK

———

In the days before the United States sent **Neil Armstrong** and **Buzz Aldrin** to the moon, calls for justice were ringing out in the streets of New York City. The year was 1969. Only five years had elapsed since the Civil Rights Act of 1964 became law and prohibited discrimination based on race, color, religion, sex, or national origin in public institutions. Unfortunately, even as landmark civil rights legislation sought to provide legal protections to **marginalized groups**, little had changed. For America's people of color, women, **LGBTQ** individuals, and those at the intersections, the era that took man to the moon did not bring lasting change for everyone.

In spite of this, a number of leaders were paving the way for acceptance of all people and changing the cultural conversation about race, **gender**, and civil rights. These pioneers became some of the first women of color to advance in their fields—engineers and mathematicians, policy makers, Broadway playwrights, and activists. Even as forces of discrimination—like **segregation** and hate—worked against them, these dynamic women made important efforts to advance equality, and without their work, the efforts of today's activists might not be possible.

To truly understand the accomplishments of these women, it is imperative to understand the institutional barriers they fought against and the historical context from which they emerged. We all hold a piece of the puzzle to changing the world for the better. As we fight against oppression like our foremothers, we can envision a future where everyone can reach the stars. In "Laying the Groundwork," we will learn about activists, cultural icons, elected officials, and scientists of the mid-twentieth century whose work laid the foundations of modern-day activist movements.

SYLVIA RIVERA & MARSHA P. JOHNSON

SILL-vee-ah ree-VAIR-ah / MAR-shah JON-sun

In 1969, the modern Lesbian, Gay, Bisexual, Transgender, and Queer (LGBTQ) Rights Movement was born at the Stonewall Inn in New York City. At the helm of the movement were two transgender women of color, Marsha P. Johnson and Sylvia Rivera. These revolutionaries fought for LGBTQ equality at a time when the American Psychological Association considered homosexuality to be a mental illness. Even within the movement that the two made lifelong efforts to advance, Marsha and Sylvia were cast to the margins of the community and largely erased from its history.

> "I'm not missing a minute of this— it's the revolution!"
> –Sylvia Rivera

Marsha P. Johnson was born on August 24, 1945, in Elizabeth, New Jersey, and lived at the intersection of transgender, queer, and black identity. Like many LGBTQ people of color, she was the target of discrimination and police violence. Sylvia Rivera was born on July 2, 1951, in New York City. Forced out of her home by homophobic relatives at age eleven, Sylvia lived on the streets of Times Square, where she had to constantly dodge imminent threats of violence. She faced anti-LGBTQ discrimination throughout her life but she refused to be anyone but herself. At the age of twelve, while experiencing homelessness, she found a lifelong friend in Marsha P. Johnson, who had faced similar hardships as an LGBTQ young person. Like Marsha, Sylvia began engaging in sex work during adolescence to survive. LGBTQ youth of color are more likely to experience poverty and homelessness because of combined forces of racism, anti-LGBTQ discrimination, and the lack of dedicated resources. The struggles that Marsha and Sylvia fought against fueled a passion within them to provide shelter and resources to LGBTQ youth experiencing homelessness, a dream that they would work their entire lives to manifest.

These two budding activists were only twenty-three and seventeen when the Stonewall Riots took place. These riots started on the night of June 28, 1969, with an encounter between local police and the patrons at the Stonewall Inn in New York City's West Village. Police entered the Stonewall Inn to intimidate and harass the bar's guests. Patrons like Sylvia Rivera carried with them years of trauma from police violence and confronted the blatant injustice with righteous fury. The night of resistance escalated into a full-scale protest and many people were brutalized and jailed during their fight for respect. The Stonewall Riots were the catalyst for an entirely new era of LGBTQ resistance, born out of a rejection of respectability, police violence, and discrimination. Today, the LGBTQ community pays homage to the uprising at the Stonewall Inn with annual Pride marches and parades.

Following the Stonewall Riots, Sylvia became a founding member of the Gay Liberation Front and the Gay Activists Alliance, which advocated for LGBTQ civil rights. The following year, Marsha and Sylvia founded Street Transvestite Action Revolutionaries (STAR), which worked to protect transgender youth from the hardships of homelessness and poverty. They opened STAR House as a safe space and shelter for LGBTQ youth experiencing homelessness in New York City.

> "As long as gay people don't have their rights all across America, there's no reason for celebration."
> —Marsha P. Johnson

Despite being committed to LGBTQ liberation, both activists were often silenced and shoved out of their own movement because of discrimination against gender-nonconforming people. Nevertheless, they would not be stopped. In 1973, Sylvia gave a harrowing speech at a women's liberation rally in New York City. Fighting for the right to be heard, she seized her place on the stage and called out the numerous failures of the women's rights and gay and lesbian liberation movements to acknowledge and protect transgender women of color and incarcerated members of the LGBTQ community. With her voice and her powerful truth, Sylvia Rivera moved an entire audience to recognize her humanity and the struggles faced by trans and gender-nonconforming people. She would continue speaking up and advocating on these issues until her death. Marsha dedicated the rest of her life to bringing awareness to the HIV/AIDS crisis in New York City, working with ACT UP! to continue to fight for freedom.

Fifty years after Stonewall, the erasure of and violence toward transgender women of color continues. Today, Marsha and Sylvia's legacies are carried on by transgender women of color like Jennicet Gutiérrez and Raquel Willis. Like their foremothers, these organizers refuse to be silenced and pushed to the margins of the liberation movements that they helped create, and are tireless in their pursuit of civil rights, safety, and dignity for the LGBTQ community.

LORRAINE HANSBERRY

loh-RAIN HANZ-berry

Lorraine Hansberry was born on May 19, 1930, in Chicago, Illinois, to civil rights activist parents. In the mid-1930s, the Hansberry family moved to a predominantly white housing development where they were harassed relentlessly. One night, Lorraine and her sister, Mamie, were sitting in the living room when a concrete block was hurled at them through the window. In addition to physical intimidation, the family faced legal action by white homeowners who wanted the courts to force the Hansberrys to move. The battle went to the Supreme Court and ultimately the Hansberrys won. Lorraine, only ten years old at the time of the case, learned the power of standing up for her rights.

As a young adult, Lorraine moved to New York City and worked as an associate editor of **Paul Robeson**'s Harlem-based newspaper, *Freedom*, a political publication that openly challenged **racism** during a time of widespread media censorship.

Through her work with *Freedom*, Lorraine discovered her voice as a writer and gained exposure to a network of black creatives and intellectuals who were using art and the written word to advocate for racial justice and **LGBTQ** rights. During this period of her life, she wrote *The Crystal Stair*, a play about a black family in Chicago dealing with hardships similar to those that the Hansberry family endured during her childhood. The play was later retitled *A Raisin in the Sun* after a line from a poem by **Harlem Renaissance** poet **Langston Hughes**. Hansberry's play was revolutionary because it provided white audiences with a window into the lives of everyday black Americans facing the challenges of racism and economic inequality. For the black community, Hansberry's work was a milestone in the accurate portrayal of the black American experience at a time when **blackface** and racist caricatures were commonplace. *A Raisin in the Sun* debuted on Broadway in 1959, making it the first play produced on Broadway by a black woman. Lorraine was also the youngest American and first black playwright to win a New York Drama Critics' Circle Award.

Lorraine became a prominent and passionate activist during the early 1960s. Though she never explicitly stated her sexual orientation during her life, many scholars and organizers revere her as a black **queer feminist** leader who worked alongside well-known black LGBTQ writers like **James Baldwin** in the movement for liberation.

Though Lorraine's life was cut short by cancer in her early thirties, her legacy continues to inspire people to use their creative talents to make the stories of their families and communities heard.

PATSY TAKEMOTO MINK

PAT-see tahk-eh-MOE-toe MEENK

Patsy Takemoto Mink was born on December 6, 1927, on the island of Maui in Hawaii. Patsy was a third-generation Japanese immigrant, or *sansei*, while her parents were second-generation, or *nisei*.

Patsy grew up during World War II, and on December 7, 1941, when she was a sophomore in high school, the Japanese military attacked Pearl Harbor. As Americans grieved, including those of Japanese descent, a pervasive wave of anti-Japanese racism swept the nation. In 1942, President Franklin Delano Roosevelt signed Executive Order 9066 into law, which authorized the forced removal of people of Japanese ancestry from their homes and interned them in detention facilities across America. Because Patsy's family was not *issei*, or first-generation, they were not subjected to internment, but they experienced the xenophobia and racism of the time. As this massive violation of human rights affected the entire Japanese American community, Patsy sought to make her community a better place by forging a career in politics to advocate for equality. Her foray into elected office began as a senior in high school, when she was elected student body president, and continued meteorically throughout the rest of her career.

Patsy went on to earn a law degree and became the first Japanese American woman attorney in Hawaii. In 1964, Patsy became the first woman of color, first Asian American woman, and first woman from the state of Hawaii to be elected to the United States Congress.

Though she had advocated throughout her career for the rights of women and immigrant communities, Patsy's most enduring contribution is coauthoring and sponsoring Title IX, an amendment to the Higher Education Act, in 1972. Title IX disallowed discrimination on the basis of gender by universities and colleges that receive federal funding. The amendment made changes to both the athletic and academic arenas: before Title IX, women's and men's sports were not equally funded and there was no formal prohibition of gender-based discrimination.

Patsy continued to serve in Congress until 1977, when she was appointed by President Jimmy Carter to be the Assistant Secretary of State for Oceans and International Environmental and Scientific Affairs. Patsy then returned to Congress in 1990, and served until her death in 2002. That year, Title IX was renamed the Patsy T. Mink Equal Opportunity in Education Act in recognition of her revolutionary efforts. Patsy's advocacy and passionate commitment to women's rights made landmark changes to policy and the movement toward gender equality.

DOROTHY VAUGHAN, MARY JACKSON & KATHERINE JOHNSON

DOE-ruh-thee VAHN / MARE-ee JACK-sun / KATH-er-in JON-sun

These three trailblazing women worked for NASA during the 1940s, '50s, and '60s, an era when women were all but absent in scientific fields, and the discriminatory legislation and practices collectively known as Jim Crow still mandated the segregation of black and white Americans. These gifted scientists had to advocate tirelessly to be heard and respected as black women in the scientific community and faced considerable obstacles. Their important work and legacies serve to remind us that scientific brilliance is not exclusive to a single race, gender, or class, and that discrimination should never limit the contributions that such brilliance can give to the world.

> "I changed what I could and what I couldn't, I endured."
> –Dorothy Vaughan

Dorothy Vaughan was a mathematician and the first black supervisor at NASA. Born on September 20, 1910, in Kansas City, Missouri, Dorothy was raised in Morgantown, West Virginia. She was an honor student throughout grade school, and in 1926, graduated from Wilberforce University, an HBCU. Like Mary Jackson and Katherine Johnson, Dorothy lived in a time when educational and career opportunities for black women were scarce due to sexism, racism, and segregation.

Dorothy came to the Langley Memorial Aeronautical Laboratory in 1943, during the height of World War II. While the United States Executive Order 8802, which prohibited racial, religious, and ethnic discrimination in the country's defense industry, was enacted into law at the time of her employment, Dorothy was still forced to work in segregated conditions. Everything—from bathrooms to work stations—was separated by race, and the resources allotted to people of color were often subpar.

In the face of persistent discrimination, Dorothy tenaciously moved through the ranks despite unequal opportunity and resources to succeed, and became the first black supervisor at NASA. She remained in this key position from 1949 to 1958. Throughout her tenure, Dorothy made improvements to the work conditions for black women.

Dorothy demonstrated a deft ability to redistribute power and to uplift members of her community. In leveling the playing field, she taught her team the

In 1942, Mary graduated from the HBCU Hampton University at a time when less than 5 percent of women in the United States completed four-year college degrees. After college, she went on to teach at a school in Maryland, later serving as a bookkeeper and Army secretary.

In 1951, Mary began working at NASA as a human computer, and in 1953 she was offered a position with NASA engineer Kazimierz Czarnecki. She soon began working on a 60,000-horsepower wind tunnel called the Supersonic Pressure Tunnel. Mary's invaluable contributions to this project led her supervisors to recommend her for a promotion from mathematician to engineer. However, she could not be eligible for the promotion without an advanced degree, and the only local institution to offer the training she needed was segregated. Undeterred, Mary petitioned the city of Hampton to allow her to join her white colleagues in the classroom. She was successful, and in 1958, she became the first black woman engineer at NASA, where she worked until her retirement in 1985.

FORTRAN programming language, giving the human computers under her supervision a significant edge in the forthcoming technological age. She never took no for an answer and tirelessly advocated for the rights of her staff, paving the way for institutions like NASA to see all their employees as integral, valuable, and deserving of equal treatment, facilities, and benefits.

Mary Jackson was NASA's first black woman engineer. Born on April 9, 1921, in Hampton, Virginia, she grew up in an era when career opportunities and educational resources were scarce for people of color and women.

Katherine Johnson was born on August 26, 1918, in White Sulphur Springs, West Virginia. Gifted and highly intelligent, she graduated from high school at the age of fourteen and began attending an HBCU called West Virginia State College. She graduated from college at eighteen with degrees in mathematics and French.

Before beginning her career at NASA, Katherine was a public school teacher in Virginia and continued her education as the first black woman to attend graduate school at West Virginia University. In 1953, Katherine Johnson began working at NASA as a human computer helping to calculate the trajectory of several NASA missions.

In spite of the discrimination Katherine faced as a black woman, her calculations came to be trusted above all her colleagues' for their unmatched accuracy. In 1962, she was entrusted with confirming complex computer calculations before the launch of the Friendship 7—the third human space flight launched by the United States. This made her an important part not only of the history of civil rights but also of the US space program.

In 1958, Katherine transitioned into the Spacecraft Controls Branch when NASA integrated its workforce and began using digital computers. There, she worked to calculate the launch window for the 1961 manned Mercury mission and the flight path for the first manned mission to the moon in 1969. She worked at NASA until her retirement in 1986.

Katherine Johnson's legacy includes a thirty-three-year-long career in aerospace, twenty-six published scientific papers, and an untold number of inspired women seeking to make their mark in the fields of STEM.

CHAPTER 2

LEADING THE MOVEMENT

Intersectionality is a way of understanding the various forms of oppression in society and how they impact us according to our overlapping identities. If you are a black Muslim woman like me, you are likely to be affected by **racism**, **sexism**, and **anti-Muslim** discrimination at the same time. The theory of intersectionality was developed by black legal scholar and **feminist Kimberlé Crenshaw** in her 1989 essay, "Demarginalizing the Intersection of Race and Sex." Before this groundbreaking theory emerged, many human rights movements adhered to the idea that oppression must be fought one form at a time.

In recent years, the intersectional movement Black Lives Matter has completely transformed the organizing landscape in the United States and beyond. As social media facilitated increased coverage and awareness of violence against unarmed black people, many Americans began feeling a mix of trauma, fury, and despair. Demands for justice and accountability reached a critical mass in 2013 following the acquittal of vigilante George Zimmerman in the murder of unarmed black teen **Trayvon Martin**. Media outlets villainized Trayvon Martin and painted Zimmerman's shooting of the unarmed teen as a righteous act of self-defense. Following the news of the acquittal, activist and writer **Alicia Garza** posted a heartfelt message on Facebook: "Black people. I love you. I love us. Our lives matter, Black Lives Matter." Quickly identifying a resonant message in Alicia's post, organizer **Patrisse Cullors** shared the message and added the hashtag **#BlackLivesMatter**. At its core "Black Lives

Matter" is call to recognize and celebrate the humanity of all black people in a world that seeks to oppress and extinguish black life. Patrisse and Alicia began working with community organizer **Opal Tometi**, and in 2013 the three transformed the viral hashtag and call for justice into an organized network of activists fighting against the multiple forms of oppression faced by black people.

As a movement, Black Lives Matter is composed of everyday people and organizers who work to end the violence committed against innocent black folks. As an organization, the **Black Lives Matter Global Network** is a chapter-based, member-led organization whose mission is to build local power and to intervene in violence inflicted on black communities by the state and vigilantes. In 2016, the Black Lives Matter Global Network joined a collective of more than fifty organizations representing thousands of black people from across the United States to unveil the **Movement for Black Lives** policy platform. The intersectional policy platform provides research briefs and recommendations on over thirty policies to end violence against black, **transgender**, **queer**, immigrant, and disabled people in America. As a movement, organization, and policy platform, Black Lives Matter continues to make history by using a community-rooted and research-informed approach to fighting for liberation.

Following the results of the 2016 US presidential election, many Americans were shocked and disgusted by the triumph of **Donald Trump**. Teresa Shook, a grandmother living in Hawaii, used social media to take action and invited about forty friends to her Facebook event for a pro-women march. The next day, over ten thousand people had indicated they would be attending. **Bob Bland**, a fashion entrepreneur in Brooklyn, had a similar idea for a pro-women march. Bob and Teresa met through Facebook and decided to combine the two events.

In the early days of the **Women's March**, a lens toward intersectionality was lacking. The march's original name, "**Million Woman March**," was a thoughtless erasure of the march of the same name led by black women in 1997. As activist communities around the country expressed frustration, Vanessa Wruble recognized the lack of diversity and connected Bob Bland to a trio of experienced community organizers of color—**Tamika D. Mallory**, **Carmen Perez**, and **Linda Sarsour**—who began spearheading planning for what became the Women's March. Having worked together in social justice for years, Tamika, Carmen, and Linda leveraged their broad networks to bring in brilliant women of color to develop an intersectional policy platform that included all communities. To avoid erasing the legacy of the **1963 March on Washington**, which is remembered for the famous speech by **Dr. Martin Luther King, Jr.**, "I Have a Dream," the march organizers sought the guidance of his daughter, **Dr. Bernice King**. With her blessing, the march became known as Women's March on Washington. On January 21, 2017, five million people across the world on all seven continents attended the march and its hundreds of companion marches.

Through meaningful and thoughtful action and with an intersectional strategy, the Women's March became more than a massive demonstration—it became a movement. Immediately following the march, organizers released an initiative called "10 Actions for the First 100 Days" to transform the energy of new activists into deliberate and positive action. In its first year, Women's March activists fought alongside immigrant rights groups to protect undocumented people living in the United States, disability justice advocates for compassionate and equitable health care reform, and anti-racism advocates to reckon with the **privilege** held by **cisgender** white women.

Though it began as a theory in a legal essay, "intersectionality" proves to be an effective approach to community organizing. Black Lives Matter prioritizes the voices of women, immigrants, and **LGBTQ** people instead of adhering to the patriarchal approach of black liberation movements of the past. The Women's March rejects exclusionary feminism—which only has room for white, cisgender, heterosexual women—and brings experienced organizers from different communities together to advance justice for all women. While organizers continue to grow and evolve, the movements of today are rooted in community, receptive to critique, and guided by collective leadership. In "Leading the Movement" we will learn about the revolutionary activists, organizers, and scholars whose work and leadership have transformed the way justice is brought forth.

KIMBERLÉ CRENSHAW

KIM-bur-lee KREN-shaw

Black legal scholar, feminist, and educator Kimberlé Crenshaw is a leader in the fields of civil rights, black feminism, legal theory, race, and the law. Her work has been foundational in two fields of study that have come to be known by terms that she coined: critical race theory and intersectionality.

Born in 1959 in Canton, Ohio, Kimberlé earned her undergraduate degree at Cornell University and went on to earn her juris doctorate at Harvard in 1984. In 1985, she earned a master of laws at the University of Wisconsin.

Already an accomplished legal scholar, in 1989, Kimberlé penned the essay, "Demarginalizing the Intersection of Race and Sex" wherein she detailed the theory of intersectionality. While the term first appeared in 1989, the concept of intersectionality is not new. Racism and sexism are the reasons that we rarely hear the names of women like Diane Nash and Fannie Lou Hamer—black women leaders who were critical to the Civil Rights Movement. Kimberlé argued that the experiences of black women are erased from feminist scholarship and anti-racism discourse because there is no consideration for the overlapping or intersectional experience of being both black and a woman. As noted by Kimberlé, the erasure of black women's experiences results in black women being denied protections under the law.

In 1996, Kimberlé founded the African American Policy Forum to connect academics, activists, and policy-makers in the fight against inequality in the law. In 2011, Kimberlé and Columbia Law School established the Center for Intersectionality and Social Policy Studies to expand the research on intersectionality and for the advancement of social justice.

In 2015, Kimberlé brought the worlds of academic scholarship and grassroots activism together to launch an initiative titled Say Her Name. This initiative focuses on documenting and uplifting the stories of black women, like Sandra Bland, who had been killed by police. Say Her Name included a vigil honoring the lives of women lost to police violence, a research brief on the types of violence women of color and black women face from police and other institutions, and recommendations for ways to engage communities in conversations about black women's experiences of police violence.

Kimberlé Crenshaw has changed the way we approach social justice advocacy. The idea that individuals face multiple forms of oppression at the same time continues to inform the approach of countless activists who incorporate academic research on social inequality into their organizing strategy, and employ coalition building, or bringing multiple groups together, to fight institutional barriers.

ALICIA GARZA

ah-LEE-see-ah GAR-sah

Alicia Garza was born on January 4, 1981 and raised in Northern California. Alicia began her advocacy in middle school, working to ensure her Bay Area classmates had access to information about reproductive health and contraception.

Alicia studied anthropology and sociology at UC San Diego, where she also continued her on-campus organizing and advocacy. After college, Alicia became an organizer at a fair housing organization in the Bay Area, and at twenty-three years old, she came out to her family as a queer woman. In 2009, while serving as the Executive Director of POWER (People Organized to Win Employment Rights), she began pursuing a masters in ethnic studies at San Francisco State University. At POWER, Alicia achieved a myriad of policy wins including fair housing development practices, free public transportation for young people, and the rollback of discrimination against undocumented immigrants.

"Black people. I love you. I love us. Our lives matter, Black Lives Matter."

Deeply connected to networks of community organizers and activists, it was within this context that Alicia penned the words "Black Lives Matter" in a Facebook post in 2013 after seeing the jarring news that Trayvon Martin's killer, George Zimmerman, was acquitted. With roots in racial justice, fair housing, and LGBTQ rights organizing, Alicia joined forces with Patrisse Cullors and Opal Tometi to build a base of organizers dedicated to fighting the violence and oppression faced by all black people. As commentators and activists began ignoring the truth behind Black Lives Matter—and as detractors began using the phrase "all lives matter" to derail the conversation—Alicia wrote "A Herstory of the #BlackLivesMatter Movement" for the *Feminist Wire* in 2014. In the essay, Alicia called out the theft of black queer women's work and emphasized the importance of acknowledging the foundation upon which other movements stand.

For her efforts in advancing justice for LGBTQ, black, immigrant, and marginalized communities Alicia has been awarded countless honors including the Sydney Peace Prize and Bayard Rustin Community Activist Award. She continues to fight for justice with grassroots organizations including the National Domestic Workers Alliance, which advocates for labor rights and dignity for thousands of domestic workers who are denied basic labor protections like paid leave and minimum wage.

PATRISSE CULLORS

pa-TREE-ss CULL-erz

Patrisse Cullors was born on June 20, 1983, and raised in Los Angeles, California. With three sisters and five brothers, Patrisse grew up watching her mother work to lift the family out of poverty and provide security for her children. Many of Patrisse's life-changing experiences occurred in 1999 when she was sixteen years old and moved out of her family home. At this age, Patrisse had her first girlfriend and embarked on a path of self-discovery as a **queer** black young person. She stepped into a network of **LGBTQ** organizers and found support in the words of **bell hooks** and **Audre Lorde**. The reality of **police violence** cast a shadow over Patrisse's adolescence when her older brother, Monte, was charged with evading the police and was mercilessly brutalized during his forty-month prison sentence. Seeing the injustices faced by both the LGBTQ and black communities deeply affected her as a young person and informs her organizing focus today.

After high school, she attended community college in Santa Monica and began serving as a youth mentor in the Los Angeles Unified School District. All the while, Patrisse continued her community organizing work, and at the age of twenty-two won the Mario Savio Young Activist Award for her efforts. In 2012, Patrisse received her degree in religion and philosophy from UCLA and curated her first performance art piece that fearlessly addressed the violence of incarceration, *STAINED: An Intimate Portrayal of State Violence*. In touring *STAINED*, Patrisse was inspired to form the Coalition to End Sheriff Violence and eventually started her nonprofit **Dignity & Power Now**.

In 2013, she began working with **Alicia Garza** and **Opal Tometi** to create an organizing framework around Black Lives Matter, which has revolutionized movements the world over.

Patrisse's work has improved conditions for incarcerated people in Los Angeles jails and her tenacity as an organizer has inspired countless young people to become champions of social justice. However, the visibility that Patrisse has earned also places her at risk of surveillance, a topic which she discusses at length in her first book, *When They Call You a Terrorist: A Black Lives Matter Memoir* (2018), which she cowrote with journalist **asha bandele**, and which has a foreword written by activist and scholar **Dr. Angela Davis**. As a world-renowned organizer and scholar, Patrisse continues to take action toward liberation through Dignity & Power Now and to speak truth to power in dialogues across the globe at institutions of higher learning.

OPAL TOMETI

OH-pull toe-MEH-tee

Born on August 15, 1984, Opal Tometi is a Nigerian American writer, community organizer and cofounder of the Black Lives Matter movement and Black Lives Matter Global Network. Growing up at the intersections of black and immigrant identity, she experienced the dual forces of anti-blackness and xenophobia early on. When Opal was sixteen, her best friend's widowed mother was deported. Despite the fact that the mother had four daughters to care for, the immigration system forced the four girls to navigate life without their mother. Fortunately, Opal's family welcomed the siblings into their home, but the experience left an indelible mark on Opal. As some of Opal's relatives also faced deportation, she became acutely aware that undocumented immigrants deserved better resources for advocacy and that she could be a driving force for change.

Opal holds a degree in history and a master's degree in communication and advocacy from the University of Arizona. Dedicated to fighting for the rights of all immigrants, Opal works to broaden the narratives around immigration beyond those that rely on stereotypes. In addition to being a transnational activist, Opal works with communities in Los Angeles, Phoenix, New York City, Oakland, Washington, D.C., and throughout the southern United States. Her activism focuses on bringing an end to police violence, immigrant detention, and domestic violence.

In the early days of the Black Lives Matter movement, Opal used her communications expertise to create its online platform and social media strategy, which gave structure to the quickly expanding movement. Since this pivotal moment in her activism, Opal continues to strategize against anti-immigrant laws across the United States. She has also worked as a caseworker for survivors of domestic violence and has served as the head of the United States' foremost black organization for immigrant rights, the Black Alliance for Just Immigration.

In addition to being honored by *Essence* magazine and the *Los Angeles Times*, Opal is featured in the Smithsonian's National Museum of African American History and Culture, and in 2016 she received the first ever Webby Award for Social Movement of the Year alongside Black Lives Matter cofounders Patrisse Cullors and Alicia Garza.

CARMEN PEREZ

CAR-men peh-REZ

Born on January 21, 1977, Carmen Perez grew up in Oxnard, California, a farming community outside of Los Angeles. Basketball became her outlet to escape the gang and **police violence** in her community. The violence within Carmen's community was fueled by President **Ronald Reagan's War on Drugs**, which increased the number of people incarcerated for nonviolent drug offenses from 50,000 in 1980 to more than 400,000 by 1997. At seventeen, the death of her nineteen-year-old sister became a catalyst for Carmen to pursue a path of social justice. She became dedicated to transforming the lives of young people, and aspired to reduce the violence happening in her community and around the world.

After earning her bachelor's degree in psychology from UC Santa Cruz in 2001, Carmen began working for **Barrios Unidos**, an organization dedicated to providing nonviolence training and reentry services for formerly incarcerated individuals. While working at Barrios Unidos, Carmen was recruited by the Santa Cruz County Probation Department to be a probation officer. Soon she began implementing trauma-informed programming for young women facing incarceration and advocating for alternatives to detention, such as therapy.

In 2005, she met **Harry Belafonte** and joined the founding team of **The Gathering for Justice**, which connects cultural icons with networks of community organizers and activists to educate the larger public about legislative and policy initiatives. In 2008, Carmen became the national organizer of The Gathering for Justice, and in 2010, she was promoted to executive director of the organization.

In 2014, Carmen was already working alongside fellow activists **Linda Sarsour** and **Tamika D. Mallory** to speak out against the murder of Staten Island grandfather **Eric Garner** at the hands of NYPD Officer Daniel Pantaleo. In 2016, the three leaders joined **Bob Bland** to cochair the **Women's March**, which took place on Carmen's birthday in 2017.

Carmen focuses her life's work at the **intersectionality** of numerous human rights issues, including mass incarceration, **gender** equality, violence prevention, and police accountability. She has been honored by many organizations for her work, including the **NAACP** and **National Action Network**.

> "What we really want is for violence to stop! We want for police officers to be held accountable the same way we as civilians are held accountable."

LINDA SARSOUR

LIN-dah sar-SOOR

Linda Sarsour is a Palestinian American Muslim activist and a dedicated advocate of peace and justice. Born in March 1980 to Palestinian immigrant parents, Linda grew up in Brooklyn, New York.

Linda's commitment to community drew her to work across religious affiliation, racial heritage, and country of origin. Her intercommunity activism in New York City had new meaning following the September 11, 2001 terrorist attacks. As the media conversations following the attack became increasingly anti-Muslim and xenophobic, Americans began to turn against the Muslim community. In the wake of hatred, Linda continued to speak up for justice as a visible Muslim woman who observes hijab. Her bold and vocal commitment to liberation defied the biases of many Americans who believe that Muslim women are victims of a repressive faith. Prior to her rise to national prominence as a leader of the Women's March, Linda worked to help curb the unwarranted surveillance of New York's Muslim communities and applied political pressure against the racist policing tactic called "stop and frisk."

Linda is a member of Justice League NYC, a leading force of activists, formerly incarcerated individuals, and artists working to reform the New York Police Department and the criminal justice system. She has also served many civil rights organizations including as executive director of the Arab American Association of New York, and as cofounder of the first online Muslim organizing platform, MPOWER Change.

In 2016, Linda became a cochair of the Women's March on Washington and rose to prominence on a national stage. As President Donald Trump's policies like the Muslim ban turned Americans against their Muslim neighbors and reenergized the xenophobia of the early 2000s, Linda became a target of sexist and anti-Muslim harassment online and in the media. Against waves of intense hatred, Linda Sarsour continues to be an outspoken role model, not only for Muslim women, but for budding activists from all walks of life.

She has received numerous awards and honors, including "Champion of Change" from the Obama White House. With her fellow Women's March cochairs, she was named one of *Time* magazine's "100 Most Influential People in the World," and one of *Fortune* magazine's "World's Greatest Leaders."

In the presence of seemingly endless harassment, Linda Sarsour continues to be a freedom fighter working everyday toward the collective liberation of all people.

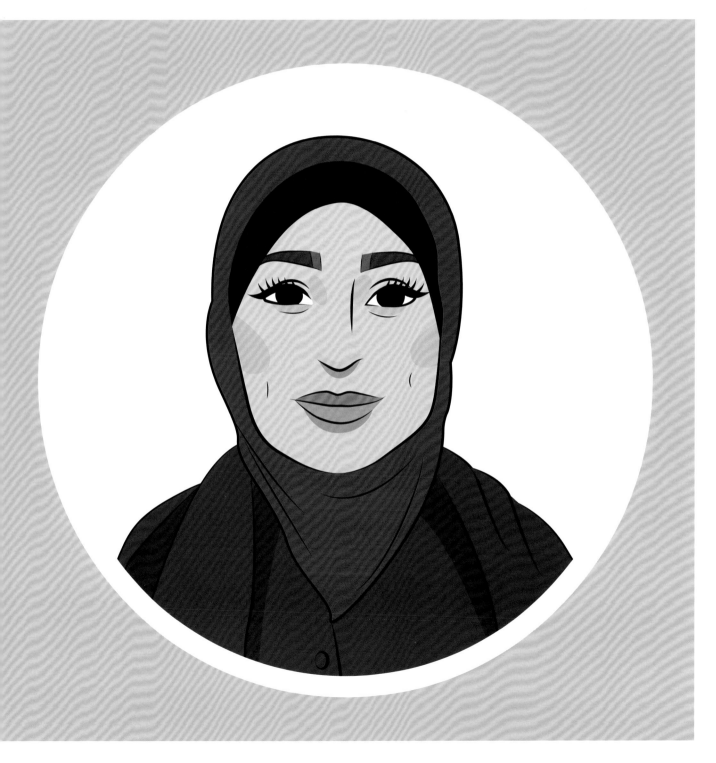

TAMIKA D. MALLORY

tah-MEE-kah DEE MAL-oh-ree

Born in 1980 in Harlem, New York, Tamika D. Mallory's life was influenced by community organizing from a young age. Her parents were early members of Reverend Al Sharpton's civil rights organization, the National Action Network (NAN). At eleven, Tamika also joined the network as a member because of its community-rooted approach to solving issues happening in her own backyard. By fifteen she was a volunteer staff member at NAN, and in 2011, she became the organization's youngest-ever executive director, having worked for the organization for over a decade.

At the age of twenty, a tragic event shook Tamika's life when the father of her young son had his life cut short by gun violence in 2001. This personal experience became a catalyst for an increased focus in her advocacy work. After the 2012 mass shooting at Sandy Hook Elementary that took the lives of twenty children, the Obama Administration created a Gun Violence Task Force under the leadership of Vice President Joe Biden. At the time, Tamika was the executive director of NAN and was asked to serve on the task force, bringing with her years of experience working in the gun violence prevention movement. While the task force was established in the wake of a mass shooting, Tamika emphasized the need to create solutions to gun violence that would address not just mass shootings but also pervasive everyday gun violence. During this time, President Barack Obama's senior advisor, Valerie Jarrett, called Tamika a "leader of tomorrow," based on her relentless drive in championing the needs and demands of her community.

In continued activism, she served as a national organizer for the fiftieth anniversary of the March on Washington in 2013, which drew 300,000 attendees, as well as Justice or Else! in 2015, where she delivered a national address to over 700,000 attendees. In New York City, Tamika was instrumental in creating the NYC Crisis Management System, an official gun violence prevention program that awards nearly $20 million annually to innovative violence prevention organizations. In 2017, Tamika D. Mallory made history alongside Linda Sarsour, Bob Bland, and Carmen Perez when she became a national cochair of the historic Women's March.

Today, Tamika continues to fight for a more just world. Despite the flurry of forces hoping to silence her, she persists.

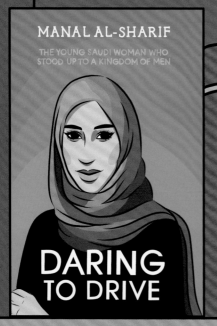

SPEAKING TRUTH
TO POWER

Storytelling is a central part of what it means to be human. No matter how boring the plotline or the messenger, we are hardwired to stick around for the end of a story once it's begun. Stories can inspire change and empower people. That is why **Edward Bulwer-Lytton**'s quote, "The pen is mightier than the sword," is so resonant. However, bigoted leaders can also use storytelling to obscure the truth and advance false narratives that inspire violence and hatred against entire communities. The communities in the crosshairs are denied the access and opportunity to speak up and are then expected to be silent. Despite the expectation of silence, trailblazing heroes are speaking truth to power and going against the dominant narratives that inaccurately portray their realities. Revolutionary writers and communicators use the written word to empower young people and those outside of the white **heteronormative** mainstream to believe in themselves and to forge a path forward to a better future. This battle to speak truth to power is taking place simultaneously while organizers and movement leaders dismantle unjust institutions. Through the written and spoken word, diverse communities are fighting for visibility in a society that continues to demand silence from those outside of the status quo.

In the United States and in countries around the world, serious backlash and **harassment** can result for those who dare to speak against the real injustice happening in their communities. Through vocal opposition, activists confront those who would rather cling to a warped view of the world than face a flawed yet diverse and vibrant reality. By speaking up, social justice activists and leaders worldwide risk their very lives and security to change conversations and destigmatize taboo topics like race, **gender**, body image, and ability. Through storytelling, activists can pursue measurable policy change, increased representation, shifts in empathy, and more.

In "Speaking Truth to Power," we will learn about leaders who have written revolutionary books, undertaken bold acts of defiance, and changed institutions to provide a more holistic worldview and integrate diverse communities into the story of humanity.

ALLISON RENVILLE

AL-ih-sun REN-vill

Allison Renville is a Native American human-rights activist and organizer. Born on June 12, 1984, Allison lives within Traverse des Sioux Treaty Territory in northeastern South Dakota where her family has lived since their removal from their original homelands, which are now known as the Twin Cities Metro Area in Minnesota. Allison is the great-great maternal granddaughter of Chief Gabriel "TiWakan" Renville of the Sisseton Wahpeton Oyate. As a direct descendant of a leader of her people, she has always been intimately connected to her heritage and community and felt tremendous love and pride for her culture.

In her early twenties, Allison volunteered with Obama for America and became a campaign captain in her home district. With her help, the campaign was able to secure six of the eleven delegate points necessary to win a majority in the Democratic primary, securing Barack Obama's nomination as the democratic candidate for president in 2008.

In 2016, local Standing Rock Sioux Nation tribal members put out a call to take action against the construction of the Dakota Access Pipeline (DAPL), a 1,172-mile underground oil pipeline cutting across North Dakota, South Dakota, Iowa, and Illinois. The pipeline would harm sacred tribal sites and place the primary water supply of the Standing Rock Sioux Reservation at risk of contamination.

As a tribal member of Standing Rock Sioux Nation herself, Allison arrived two days after the initial call for protest. Peaceful protesters began occupying an encampment in the DAPL construction path and in August, brutal arrests of those practicing civil disobedience began. From August 2016 to January 2017, Allison lived within the encampment and participated in the months-long peaceful protests against the pipeline. Online and traditional media conversations about the protests failed to accurately portray the priorities and concerns of people on the ground. As a skilled political organizer, Allison began writing about her experiences at Standing Rock and conducted interviews with prominent outlets including NPR, NBC, Reuters, and more. She used traditional media to shift the narrative from one of misinformation to one that highlighted the prayers of tribal members, the struggles they faced, and the expectations they demanded of the presidential administration.

Today, Allison is working on launching a political action committee and beginning her foray into elected office in South Dakota.

BRITTANY PACKNETT

BRIT-nee PACK-net

Brittany Packnett was born on November 12, 1984, and raised in St. Louis, Missouri. Brittany's lifelong commitment to social justice stems from her Christian upbringing. As the daughter of a pastor and an ordained Baptist minister, Brittany attended weeknight Bible studies and learned about the legacy of Jesus Christ. For Brittany, Jesus represented a figure who fought for liberation and justice of all people unconditionally.

Remaining connected to her hometown community, Brittany attended St. Louis's Washington University where she studied African and African American studies. In 2014, while Brittany served as the executive director of Teach for America in St. Louis, an unarmed black eighteen-year-old named Michael Brown was murdered by police in nearby Ferguson on August 9. In response to this horrific act in her own community, Brittany became an active participant in the demonstrations in Ferguson to protest the failures of local government and the proliferation of police violence. These protests went on for over five months and brought national attention to the daily injustices and threats of violence faced by black young people. Brittany used Twitter and other social media to counter the distorted media narratives about the protests in Ferguson and soon became a prominent part of the collective online community known colloquially as Black Twitter, lending her voice to important issues like access to education, voting rights, and equal pay.

During the summer of 2015, Packnett cofounded Campaign Zero, a policy platform designed to end police violence, and she has since continued to dedicate both her life and career to the advancement of justice. As someone intimately connected to the realities of police violence in her hometown of St. Louis, Brittany was also appointed to President Barack Obama's Task Force on 21st Century Policing in 2015 at the height of the national crises around state violence. In 2016, she became the Vice President of National Community Alliances at Teach for America and crafted the organization's first civil rights and equity agenda.

As a result of her work, Brittany has been recognized as an important figure in the movement for positive social change. Today, she continues to advocate for urgent systemic change at critical decision-making tables and through national and international media. Her organizing prowess is matched by her commitment to recognizing and elevating young leaders into crucial conversations and opportunities.

GERALDINE ROMAN

JER-ul-deen ROE-mun

In 2016, Geraldine Roman became the first openly transgender elected official in the history of the Philippines. Fiercely dedicated to the human rights of all people, no matter who they are or where they are from, Geraldine uses her position and access to forge a better future for all.

Born in 1967, Geraldine is the second of four children and was raised in Orani, Bataan. Geraldine grew up in a political family: her mother, Herminia Roman, served nine years as a congresswoman in the seat Geraldine would later occupy, a seat previously held by Geraldine's late father, Antonino Roman, Jr. As an LGBTQ youth living in a conservative Catholic country, Geraldine's childhood experiences of pushing back against bullies taught her to stand up for herself and her beliefs. To this day, Geraldine goes against convention by being a devout Catholic and committed advocate of LGBTQ equality.

While her family's legacy was deeply rooted in public service, Geraldine's first career was in journalism as the senior editor of the Spanish News Agency in Spain. As a journalist, she was able to master the power of storytelling to build empathy and understanding.

Inspired by her faith and her parents' legacy of public service, Geraldine returned to the Philippines in 2012 to embark on a career in politics with the aim of improving the lives of all people. Her debut into the political realm came when she announced her bid for the House of Representatives, running as the Liberal Party's candidate. Her platform focused on making improvements to health care, social infrastructure, and other public services.

In the Philippines, as in many countries, public policy is influenced by interpretations of religious doctrine to the detriment of LGBTQ people. In May 2016, voters of the first district of Bataan overwhelmingly chose progress and elected Geraldine Roman with a landslide 62 percent of the vote. She won at a time when transgender women of color are one of the most targeted groups globally, and she made history as the first openly transgender elected official in the history of the Philippines.

Geraldine's focus is to improve the lives of her constituents. While conservative politicians seek to thwart progress, Geraldine is a bold and vocal champion of the people moving forward with anti-discrimination legislation, equal employment opportunity legislation, and increased resources to veterans and caregivers.

JAMILAH LEMIEUX

jah-MILL-ah lah-MEW

Jamilah Lemieux was born on July 22, 1984, in Chicago, Illinois. Her father was a member of the **Black Panther Party** and her mother was active with the **Student Nonviolent Coordinating Committee.** While many of her friends and classmates were sheltered from the hard truths of black and African American history in the United States, Jamilah was well-versed in the history and legacy of slavery and black liberation movements from the time she was a young child. Jamilah's heritage as a black woman and child of community activists became a source of pride as she came to understand how her enslaved and disenfranchised ancestors fought and survived even in the face of hate, violence, and terror.

> "I don't see this country's attitudes around race, sexuality and culture changing in the way that they need to in my lifetime, but I think we can scratch the surface."

Jamilah was only eight years old when Supreme Court Justice **Clarence Thomas** was accused of sexual **harassment** by **Anita Hill** during his 1991 confirmation hearings. Though she was a child, Jamilah recognized how race and **gender** impacted the outcome of the controversial proceedings. While some felt that a powerful black man was being attacked unfairly, he still benefited from **patriarchy**, while Anita Hill was widely dismissed. Jamilah was moved by Anita Hill's bravery, and the story influenced her commitment to understanding and challenging the ways black women are punished by society for living at the intersection of **racism** and **sexism**, a commitment she upholds today through her career as a writer and activist.

Jamilah graduated from Howard University, an **HBCU** in Washington, D.C., where she studied acting. Jamilah began her writing career through blogging and soon entered the world of mainstream print media. After serving as the editor of *Ebony* magazine for several years, Jamilah took a role at iOne Digital, a black-owned media company where she launched a new millennial media brand, Cassius. Throughout her career, Jamilah has been able to tell and elevate the stories of her people, by and for her people, without having to sacrifice her integrity, identity, or truth. And she continues to dedicate her work to creating and stewarding content created by black writers and artists for a black audience.

As a commentator on major television networks and as a leader in the field of social and digital media, Jamilah speaks truth to power by challenging **rape culture**, sexism, and online harassment.

JANET MOCK

Transgender feminist author and activist Janet Mock was born in Honolulu, Hawaii, on March 10, 1983, and was raised with influences from both her African American and Native Hawaiian cultures. Janet grew up in poverty and experienced sexual abuse early in life. Despite these challenges, she made a commitment to express her authentic self, and at the age of fifteen, she named herself after Janet Jackson. By her second year of high school, and despite backlash, Janet was living her truth full-time as a young transgender woman. She went on to study at the University of Hawaii at Manoa and earn a master's in journalism from New York University.

Through her writing and activism, Janet has become a force of revolution for young trans people everywhere who are coming into their truth. In 2012, Janet started the hashtag #GirlsLikeUs, and it has since taken off as a means for trans women to share and amplify each other's stories. In 2013, she started the hashtag #TransBookDrive, an annual campaign that centralizes the stories of transgender people and donates resources to members of the trans community. With the 2014 release of her groundbreaking and *New York Times* best-selling book, *Redefining Realness*, Janet became one of the first transgender authors to give voice to the experiences of black transgender youth through her personal story and bring that story into the mainstream. Following the book's success, Janet was interviewed by Oprah Winfrey for Super Soul Sunday, making her a household name. Her second book, 2017's *Surpassing Certainty*, provides an intimate window into the realities of her life as a woman during the years in her life when she was not public about being transgender. Janet's work is crucial because she brings forth her own unique experiences as a transgender woman and empowers others to share their experiences as well. However, her boldness and her very existence draw backlash from TERFs or trans-exclusionary "radical" feminists who refuse to accept her womanhood. Nonetheless, transgender women are women, and those who claim otherwise need to unpack their biases.

An important figure in contemporary intersectional feminism, Janet Mock joined the stage as a speaker at the Women's March in 2017. Following in the footsteps of activists like Sylvia Rivera, she made a call to the millions who had gathered for a movement that uplifts all women.

KEAH BROWN

KEE-ah BROWN

Keah Brown is a black disability justice activist and journalist who uses her mastery of the written word to share stories and initiate conversations. Born on September 19, 1991, in Lockport, New York, Keah grew up in a big supportive family. Because of the large presence of strong and loving women in her family, discussions about menstruation and puberty were not taboo. This positive **feminist** environment paved the way for Keah's activism.

> "I don't want to see disability as this thing always to be pitied because it's something that I live with every day."

Keah has **cerebral palsy.** Her disability affects the motor skills on the right side of her body in addition to her reaction time. Growing up with a disability, Keah struggled to accept herself and rarely saw people she could identify with in mainstream media. It felt like she was living in a world that was actively erasing and ignoring people like her, and as such, representation became central to her activism.

With a focus toward creating more stories about people like her, Keah earned her bachelor's degree in journalism with a minor in creative writing from the State University of New York at Fredonia. During her sophomore year, she began writing for her college newspaper, and following her graduation, Keah published her first essay on a website called *Femsplain*. As a journalist, Keah has interviewed actors and scholars like **Dr. Roxane Gay**, and has been widely published in outlets such as *Essence*, *Harper's Bazaar*, and *Teen Vogue*.

In February 2017, Keah created the hashtag **#DisabledAndCute**. The hashtag encouraged disabled people around the world to affirm and celebrate themselves. In a society that portrays the disability community as a grim monolithic, #DisabledAndCute is a necessary move toward a future that uplifts everyone. For Keah, thriving and celebrating her disabled body unapologetically is an act of revolution and inspires others to celebrate themselves as well. In her 2019 essay collection *The Pretty One*, Keah bares her reality as a disabled black woman living in a world that would prefer to erase her. Like activists **Imani Barbarin** and **Mia Ives-Rublee**, Keah fights every single day to survive and adapt in an often-inaccessible environment and this fight for her existence is revolutionary.

MANAL AL-SHARIF

mun-AL ash-sha-REEF

Manal al-Sharif was born on April 25, 1979, into a Muslim family in Mecca, Saudi Arabia. Like many women and girls around the world, Manal was made to feel like her gender was a burden due to the sexist laws and prioritization of men over women. Paternalistic laws in many parts of the world, including America, reinforce the perceived weakness of femininity and deny women their humanity.

Manal graduated from King Abdulaziz University with a bachelor of science in computing and went on to work in the predominantly male field of computer technology, where, as a woman, she struggled to make her way. She was shamed for talking to her male colleagues and was required to be chaperoned by her younger brother on business trips. As a woman, she was forbidden from driving her own vehicle by the laws in Saudi Arabia. Propaganda to justify these laws ranged from myths about the health consequences of women driving to abstract interpretations of religious texts. Eventually, Manal could no longer tolerate these injustices.

In 2011, feminist Saudi Arabian activist Wajeha al-Huwaider filmed Manal driving in a defiant act of protest. The two women shared the video on YouTube and it quickly went viral on a global scale. By driving, Manal was going against the decades-long ban and joining a legacy of Saudi women activists who had been protesting the ban since the 1990s. As a result of her protest, the Saudi government arrested and imprisoned her for nine days.

The viral video of Manal driving changed the conversation around women's rights in Saudi Arabia and brought the injustice into the purview of the international human rights community. To escape the backlash that spawned from her righteous act of defiance, Manal left her home country but continued to support the efforts of Saudi Arabian women's rights activists who were fighting for their own liberation. In 2012, she was awarded the Václav Havel Prize for Creative Dissent at the Oslo Freedom Forum. *Time* magazine named her one of the "100 Most Influential People in the World," and the United Nations Human Rights Commissioner hailed her as "A Driving Force for Change" in 2013. On September 26, 2017, the ban on women drivers in Saudi Arabia was finally lifted.

In 2017, Manal's memoir, *Daring to Drive*, was published, wherein she gave an intimate view into her life's journey. She has remained a vocal women's rights activist using the written word to call attention to unjust incarceration, violence against women, and human rights atrocities globally.

ROKHAYA DIALLO

rock-HI-ya dee-ALL-oh

Born on April 10, 1978, in Paris, France, to Senegalese Muslim immigrants, Rokhaya Diallo learned to stand up for her beliefs at a young age. The diversity of her hometown sheltered Rokhaya from the realities of anti-black racism and Islamophobia that she would face later in life. While studying international and European law, Rokhaya began to experience the forces of discrimination she had been sheltered from in her youth. Despite being a proud French woman, suddenly her predominantly white peers began to ask her about her "true" origin. The daily frustration of these microaggressions inspired Rokhaya to speak out about the racism, xenophobia, and Islamophobia that plagues society.

In 2007 Rokhaya founded an anti-racism organization called Les Indivisibles (The Indivisibles), and continued speaking out about the issues of racism and xenophobia in France. Her activism caught the attention of media outlets, and soon she joined major news outlets including BET France. She became best known for her radical approach to storytelling, which provided viewers and listeners with a transparent view of global politics and racism.

In 2013, she produced the award-winning documentary, *The Steps to Liberty*, for the French TV channel France Ô. The documentary explores the journey of black American activists as they learn about the 1983 March for Equality and Against Racism, the first French anti-racist mobilization, in addition to the current state of discrimination and racism in France.

As Rokhaya gained prominence in traditional and social media, she faced countless threats of violence. Undeterred, she produced a documentary for French television that investigates the rise of hate speech and the nuances of freedom of speech online called *Networks of Hate.*

Rokhaya's 2016 documentary, *Not Yo Mama's Movement*, focuses on an emerging generation of black activists who, in the wake of the deaths of Trayvon Martin and Michael Brown, were able to seize international approval of the Black Lives Matter protests in America. The film reveals how France is confronted with similar problems of racism and police violence, the victims of which have not garnered the same media attention. Like much of Rokhaya's work, *Not Yo Mama's Movement* explores the similarities between activism in the United States and in France.

Today Rokhaya is of the most influential black activists in Europe, and her body of work has been equally praised and scrutinized for its honest examination of race, racism, and social injustice.

DR. ROXANE GAY

rocks-ANN GAY

Author and professor Dr. Roxane Gay was born on October 15, 1974, in Omaha, Nebraska. Her parents are Haitian immigrants who moved to the United States in pursuit of the American dream. Because of her family's frequent relocation for work, Roxane found comfort in books and developed a love of reading and writing at an early age. As a teen, Roxane attended the prestigious Phillips Exeter Academy and went on to graduate from Michigan Technical University with a PhD in technical communication and rhetoric. She has served as an associate professor of English at Eastern Illinois University and Purdue University.

Roxane is known for her prolific and diverse writing portfolio, and her writings are celebrated for adding depth and nuance to conversations about feminism and body image through their frank exploration of her personal history with sexual abuse, her body image, and weight. She is the author of the books *Ayiti*, *An Untamed State*, *Bad Feminist*, *Difficult Women*, and *Hunger*. She was also the author of Marvel Comics' *World of Wakanda* series, a spinoff of *Black Panther*. Her work also appears in many anthologies, and she is a contributing opinion writer for the *New York Times*.

Her critically acclaimed 2014 essay collection, *Bad Feminist*, challenges and expands the meaning of the term "feminist" while affirming the importance of personal choice in her own life. Roxane's essays envision a more inclusive feminist movement, one that recognizes LGBTQ people, women of color, and the role of privilege in feminist spaces. The book became a *New York Times* best seller and was dubbed "a manual on how to be a human" by *Time* magazine. In 2017's *Hunger*, Roxane discusses her life as a fat black woman living in a society that prioritizes thinness, whiteness, and maleness. *Hunger* is not about weight loss or conforming to conventional definitions of beauty—it's about reality.

The way Dr. Roxane Gay speaks about her personal experiences with abuse, healing, racism, and body image and combines these issues with feminist discourse and analysis has made her an incredibly influential figure in present conversations about identity, race, politics, and feminism.

> "This body is resilient. It can endure all kinds of things. My body offers me the power of presence. My body is powerful."

SANDY HO

Sandy Ho is an Asian American educator, disability justice activist, and community organizer. Born on October 1, 1987, in Boston, Massachusetts, Sandy's childhood was shaped by her thirst for knowledge. Public libraries were a sanctuary where she found independence in the ability to access information and answer her own questions about life. She was constantly reading to absorb, and writing to understand. Growing up with osteogenesis imperfecta, a condition that affects her bone development and mobility, and as someone who is hard of hearing, Sandy also wanted to figure out where she belonged within the larger disability community. As Sandy was finding her own place, she was inspired to get involved in advocacy efforts for other disabled young women.

As a college student, Sandy worked as a research assistant at the Carr Center for Human Rights at the Harvard Kennedy School of Government, and as a research associate in the area of human trafficking for Johns Hopkins University. Following college, Sandy joined AmeriCorps, completing more than 1,700 hours of community service and launching her career as a disability activist. At AmeriCorps, Sandy was tasked with developing a mentoring program for first-generation community college students, and mentorship became a high priority for her. In the years following, she created an initiative with Easter Bay Thrive Mentoring Program where disabled women from around the world share their life experiences though letters to their younger selves called "Letters to Thrive."

In the early 2010s, Sandy began writing a blog where she reflected on her experiences growing up and living with osteogenesis imperfecta, which connected her to other folks living with the condition. This led Sandy to found the Disability & Intersectionality Summit in 2016 to change the narratives around disability by focusing on people of color and women, who have historically been excluded from disability narratives and issues.

Sandy was recognized for her advocacy efforts in 2015 by the Obama Administration as a "Champion of Change" when she joined a panel discussion called "Disability Advocacy Across Generations." Today, Sandy is a professor of disability studies at her alma mater, where, in addition to teaching, she continues to fight for accessibility in education through her research and advocacy efforts, both for the students she teaches and the disability community at large.

CHAPTER 4

THE REVOLUTION WILL BE LIVE

————

The storytelling tools of film, comedy, television, and music each have the power to entertain, shift society, and build understanding. While the entertainment industry began centuries ago, the dynamic changes made in recent years reflect a transformation of human identity and culture. Through exposure to an increasingly diverse array of voices and perspectives in entertainment, millions of viewers and listeners have been able to witness the world beyond their immediate communities. But it was not always like this. Without the icons who fought to transform an entire industry, the power of film, comedy, television, and music to make change would not have been possible.

Many of these on-air and onscreen personalities came to dominate industries that did not yet exist at the time of their birth. In 1954, when **Oprah Winfrey** was born, only 55 percent of American homes had television sets, and the majority of programming was broadcast in black and white. In today's era of instant communication and twenty-four-hour news cycles, it is difficult to imagine what life was like before television, and later streaming, were commonplace. In 1971, when **Missy Elliott** was born, the music genres that she would come to dominate, rap and R&B, did not yet exist as we know them today. While music streaming services grow in popularity, many of the groundbreaking artists that fill our playlists grew up listening to records, tapes, and CDs.

Seeing cultural icons living authentically in the public eye despite the prejudices of society has empowered scores of people around the world to take pride in who they are and to follow these role models' leads. In 1986, when she was thirty-two years old, Oprah became the first black woman to host a nationally syndicated talk show. While she blazed trails and opened doors for women of color in a predominantly white industry, Oprah also brought her reality along with her. During the first season of her talk show, Oprah confronted the stigma around **sexual assault** and child abuse by coming forward as a survivor. She tore down the airbrushed filter that TV placed upon reality and made space for others to do the same. In 1997, actor and comedian **Ellen DeGeneres came out** publicly as a **lesbian** on *The Oprah Winfrey Show*, making her one of the first TV personalities to openly identify as a member of the **LGBTQ** community. Oprah and Ellen shattered expectations and conventions on national television. Both for those who were seeing themselves and their realities reflected for the first time, and those who had long benefitted from **privilege**, transformations in mass media allowed audiences to learn about aspects of the world they had never before encountered.

In "The Revolution Will Be Live," we will learn about the ways these and other cultural icons have used film, comedy, television, and music to change our social and political landscapes for the better.

AVA DUVERNAY

AY-vah DOO-ver-nay

Born on August 24, 1972, in Long Beach, California, Ava DuVernay grew up in the city of Lynwood. From a young age, Ava dedicated herself to uplifting the stories of black people and people of color.

Ava graduated with a bachelor of arts from UCLA, where she double majored in English and African American studies. After completing her undergraduate degree, she first worked as a journalist and later went on to start her own media agency dedicated to working with black entertainers.

While today Ava is an award-winning filmmaker, she didn't create her first short film until the age of thirty-two. Drawing on her adoration and knowledge of the Los Angeles hip-hop community, in 2008 she directed the critically acclaimed documentary *This Is the Life*, lauded by *LA Weekly* as "a must-see hip-hop documentary." The success of this film was just a preview of what would follow: since 2008, Ava has gone on to direct a many important features, including *Selma* (2014), *13th* (2016), and *A Wrinkle in Time* (2018). Many of her films focus on the political history of race relations in the United States, and Ava is also recognized for her commitment to opening doors for other filmmakers of color.

In 2014, Ava became the first black woman director to be nominated for a Golden Globe and to have a film, *Selma*, nominated for an Oscar for best picture. *Selma* tells the story of the student-led voting rights march of 1965 through the life of Dr. Martin Luther King, Jr., which Ava has said was inspired by her childhood summers in Alabama with her uncle, who participated in the marches.

> "If your dream only includes you, it's too small."

Ava's 2016 award-winning documentary *13th* examines race relations in the United States and reveals the depths of corruption in the American court system, a subject that had been widely discussed within academic and activist circles but had not yet become common knowledge among mainstream audiences.

Her critical successes as a filmmaker and director speak to her natural talent for storytelling, and her extensive résumé of socially conscious films separates Ava from her peers. Today, Ava continues to direct award-winning films that combine discourse and entertainment.

CAMERON ESPOSITO

CAM-run ess-poe-ZEE-toe

Originally from Chicago, Illinois, Cameron Esposito was born on October 17, 1981. Throughout her young life, Cameron reckoned with being perceived as "different." For eight years of her childhood, she had to wear an eye patch to correct her vision. This feeling of difference also emerged from Cameron's struggle to accept and embrace her sexual orientation. Growing up in a conservative religious community that lacked in diversity, she could not imagine life outside of the traditional careers and family structures with which she was familiar. Cameron used humor to fit in, a skill that would inform her career later in life.

For most of her young adulthood, Cameron participated in the performance of heterosexuality that many LGBTQ people are forced into due to society's expectations. At the age of twenty, after kissing a woman for the first time, she realized that it was okay to have these feelings and that she was a lesbian. Soon after realizing her own sexual orientation, she came out to friends and family.

Studying at Boston College and feeling emboldened by her decision to come out, Cameron began performing at improv comedy theaters near campus. Improv strengthened her signature quick and witty comedic style as she became a regular at Improv Boston and Improv Asylum. After graduating in 2006, Cameron continued her career in comedy by joining the lineup at the Lincoln Lodge in Chicago. Ironically, Cameron never imagined a future in comedy due to her conservative upbringing that emphasized getting a "real job."

From the Lincoln Lodge in Chicago, Cameron went on to perform across the country and has since become a nationally known comedian. Her comedy has received widespread critical praise, which is particularly notable given that she uses her comedic work to normalize queer identity. At its core, Cameron's activism gives license to LGBTQ individuals to celebrate themselves and to tell their stories. Her comedy album *Same Sex Symbol* and stand-up special *Marriage Material* weave her intimate personal journeys into clever punchlines, simultaneously entertaining and educating audiences. She is also the cocreator and costar of *Take My Wife*, a television series that stars Cameron and her wife, fellow comedian Rhea Butcher. In 2017, Cameron and Rhea made history by coheadlining a nationwide bus tour, Back to Back, which was the first comedy tour to feature a lesbian married couple.

CONSTANCE WU

CON-stunce WOO

Born March 22, 1982, in Richmond, Virginia, Constance Wu was one of four girls raised by parents who immigrated to the United States from Taiwan. As a child, she began performing in the local community theater scene with friends and knew early on that she wanted to pursue acting as a career. At the age of sixteen, she moved to New York to study at the famed Lee Strasberg Theatre Institute.

In 2005, Constance graduated from the State University of New York at Purchase with a degree in acting. After college, she did minor theater roles and made her screen debut in Sundance feature films including *Stephanie Daley* (2006), and *Year of the Fish* (2007). In 2010, she relocated to Los Angeles where her theater and film background earned her a role in another Sundance feature, *The Sound of My Voice* (2011).

In addition to working as an actor, Constance uses her platform to raise awareness about the lack of diversity in the media. In 2014, she was cast as Jessica Huang in the ABC comedy series, *Fresh Off the Boat*, which premiered in 2015. The series is based on the memoir of the same name by chef and TV personality Eddie Huang about growing up as a child of Asian immigrants in the 1990s. The series, which depicts a Taiwanese family living in suburban Orlando, Florida, is noted for being the first television portrayal of an Asian American family on network television in over twenty years. In the role of Jessica, Constance has contributed to showing audiences the nuances of Asian American representation. The show's popularity has provided a considerable following and platform for Constance, which she uses to directly address the directors and films guilty of practices like whitewashing, the problematic casting of white actors to play characters or historical figures that are people of color.

While Constance pursues roles that accurately depict the diversity of the Asian American experience on screen, she also advocates for the rights of women and immigrants off screen. She is a supporter of the reproductive health organization Planned Parenthood and works with Miry's List, an organization that provides essentials to newly arrived immigrant and refugee families in Southern California. Organizations like Miry's List are instrumental in helping new arrivals settle into their new lives in the United States.

ELLEN DEGENERES

ELL-en de-JEN-er-ess

Ellen DeGeneres was born on January 26, 1958, in Metairie, Louisiana. Her career in comedy began in the 1980s when she worked as an emcee at a comedy club in New Orleans. Her talent quickly led her to become a household name: in 1982, she was named Showtime's funniest person in America and in 1986 she appeared on *The Tonight Show Starring Johnny Carson*. As her comedy career boomed, she also made a name for herself in film and television, starring in the ABC sitcom *Ellen* from 1994 to 1998.

Though she knew she was gay, Ellen had remained closeted about her sexual orientation from the start of her career. In the 1980s and '90s, homophobia and stigma surrounding HIV/AIDS fueled hate violence and discriminatory policy decisions against LGBTQ people. In 1996, President Bill Clinton signed the Defense of Marriage Act, which defined marriage at the federal level as the union of one man and one woman. Against this cultural backdrop of homophobia, Ellen bravely came out on *The Oprah Winfrey Show* in 1997. Concurrently, she wrote and aired a coming out scene for the fourth season of *Ellen*, in which her character came out to a therapist played by Oprah Winfrey. The show gave millions of viewers a peek into the life of LGBTQ people who are forced to hide their true selves because of the hate and bias of society. Unfortunately, the show's network, ABC, canceled the show less than a year after Ellen became the first openly lesbian actor to play an openly lesbian character on television.

The same year the show was canceled, openly gay University of Wyoming student Matthew Shepard was beaten and left to die in a homophobic hate crime near Laramie. On October 14, 1998, just days after his death, Ellen attended a celebrity vigil on the steps of the United States Capitol where she emotionally declared, "This is what I wanted to stop. This is why I did what I did." Her heartfelt speech served as a call to action to stand with the LGBTQ community and to call for a more inclusive approach to ending hate violence.

Since September 8, 2003, Ellen has hosted her eponymous, Emmy award-winning television talk show, *The Ellen DeGeneres Show*. She also works as a voice actor, an award and game show host, and is noted for her work on behalf of humanitarian and animal rights causes. In 2016, President Barack Obama awarded her the Presidential Medal of Freedom, the United States' highest civilian honor. Today, Ellen continues to be an outspoken advocate of human and animal rights, as well as one of America's most beloved entertainers.

LESLIE JONES

LEZ-lee JONES

Leslie Jones was born on September 7, 1967, in Memphis, Tennessee. When she was a teen, her father suggested she play basketball because of her six-foot stature, and the sport became her primary focus. After high school, she went to Chapman University on a basketball scholarship and later transferred to Colorado State University.

Comedy had always been a passion of Leslie's, and though she admired comedians Lucille Ball and Carol Burnett, she had never considered being a comic herself. In 1987, a college teammate surprised Leslie by signing her up for a comedy contest. She won the contest and declared herself a comedian.

After college, Leslie moved to Los Angeles to pursue comedy and acting. From 1987 to 2010, mainstream success eluded her largely due to the industry bias against dark-skinned black women and women comedians. She continued acting in short films and performing on *Def Comedy Jam*. In 2010, Leslie filmed a comedy special called *Problem Child*, where she showcased her ability to discuss the hardships she has faced with an infectiously funny comedic flare.

In 2013, at the age of forty-seven, Leslie joined the writing staff of *Saturday Night Live*. Soon, she was serving in a dual role as a writer and an unofficial cast member. In October 2014, she officially joined the cast. Building upon the success of *Saturday Night Live*, Leslie became a fixture in pop culture and comedy following her appearance in the 2016 remake of *Ghostbusters*. As she became an increasingly visible figure, racists relentlessly targeted Leslie on social media in a barrage of slurs, threats of violence, and hacking attacks. In response to this dire situation, the digital media activist Mars Sebastian created the hashtag #LoveforLeslieJ to flood Leslie's social media pages with messages of love and support, with participation from entertainment industry leaders like Margaret Cho and Jada Pinkett Smith.

In 2016, Leslie's online comedic presence earned her a role with NBC as a commentator on the Rio Olympics. While not initially part of the Olympic programming, Jones's irreverent tweets caused audiences to clamor for her inclusion. When gymnast Gabby Douglas was bombarded with racist harassment online, Leslie stood up for her by starting the viral hashtag #Love4GabbyUSA to drown out the haters and inundate the Olympian's timeline with encouragement.

Today, Leslie continues to be a pop culture sensation. Through her comedy, social commentary, and bold presence, she gives people everywhere permission to be unapologetically themselves.

MISSY ELLIOTT

MISS-ee ELL-ee-uht

Born Melissa Arnette Elliott on July 1, 1971, Missy "Misdemeanor" Elliott had a difficult upbringing. As a child, Missy survived sexual abuse and witnessed the brutal physical abuse that her mother, Patricia, endured at the hands of her father. To cope with the traumas of her youth, Missy turned to faith, music, and humor, and discovered her talent as a musician. As a child, she would perform concerts for an audience of her toys, and she recalls putting her dolls' hands in the air and providing the roars of applause herself. Missy often wrote to her musical inspiration, Janet Jackson, for help during the hardest times of her childhood. When she was fourteen, Missy and her mother bravely escaped the abusive violence of her father. This moment of triumph was facilitated by their entire family—her mother enlisted aunts, cousins, and uncles to load up the family's possessions and move on to a new chapter of a healthier life.

Missy's music career began in 1991, when she joined an all-women R&B group called Sista. In 1996, working alongside her close friend Timbaland, a music producer and rapper, Missy wrote for emerging star Aaliyah's album *One in a Million*, which went double platinum. After that, Missy began finding her own voice as a rapper and producer. Supported by Timbaland and a strong network of black artists within the industry, Missy went on to release six studio albums that have all gone platinum or higher, making her the first woman rapper to hold such a notable distinction. But women rappers and R&B artists are rarely acknowledged for the commercial and pop culture successes they attain. While Missy has achieved major successes behind the scenes as a writer and producer and is well-known for her onstage and recording prowess, she has rarely been given the same acclaim or mainstream acknowledgment as male writers, musicians, and producers.

With Grammy nominations spanning multiple decades, Missy Elliott has become an important icon in an artistic sphere dominated by men, and has used her well-deserved successes to champion the rights of women and girls. In 2016, Missy teamed up with First Lady Michelle Obama to release the women's empowerment anthem "This Is for My Girls" in support of various campaigns centered around empowering young women. In addition to her music career, Missy is an advocate for human and animal rights. Through her work, she has shown that healing from trauma—and that being massively successful despite trauma—is achievable.

OPRAH WINFREY

OH-prah WIN-free

Oprah Winfrey was born on January 29, 1954, in rural Mississippi. Her career as a journalist began in 1971 when she enrolled in the HBCU Tennessee State University and joined the college radio station. By the time Oprah entered her twenties, she was already making history as the youngest anchor and the first black woman TV reporter with WTVF-TV in Nashville.

After graduating from college, Oprah moved to Baltimore, Maryland, where she hosted her first talk show at the age of twenty-four. At the time, she was criticized for her energetic on-screen presence and passionate delivery of news stories. But, in 1983, when she became the host of a thirty-minute talk show in Chicago, Illinois, her infectious personality and knack for storytelling earned her higher ratings than *The Phil Donahue Show*, the reigning champion of talk show television since its debut in 1970.

Soon Oprah's airtime and reach grew from the thirty-minute slot on *A.M. Chicago* to an hour-long talk show named for its host. In September 1986, when Oprah was thirty-two, *The Oprah Winfrey Show* made its national debut and made her the first black woman to host a nationally syndicated talk show.

The Oprah Winfrey Show educated Americans about a myriad of issues that had not previously been discussed in such a visible way. In November 1986, during a show about **sexual abuse**, Winfrey revealed that she herself had been a survivor of sexual abuse since the age of nine. Using her personal truth to raise awareness and give survivors a voice, Oprah also used her platform to take meaningful action for children everywhere. In 1993, she became a vocal proponent of the National Child Protection Act, also known as "The Oprah Bill." Signed into law by President **Bill Clinton**, the bill required states to report records of child abuse crimes into a national database for use during background checks of individuals seeking employment in childcare.

This act of advocacy stemming from personal experience is just one example of the way Oprah has integrated her political and social commitments into her professional life. Her warmth and authenticity, in addition to her savvy as a media mogul and generosity as a philanthropist, is what she has become known and loved for. For twenty-five years from 1986 to 2011, *The Oprah Winfrey Show* was the highest-rated television program of its kind. Following the end of the show, she launched the Oprah Winfrey Network (OWN), which takes Oprah's signature ability to turn moments of vulnerability into calls to action and opportunities for transformative education.

SERENA WILLIAMS

sur-EE-nah WILL-yumz

Serena Williams was born on September 26, 1981, in Saginaw, Michigan. Along with her older sister Venus Williams, Serena began an intense regimen of tennis training by her father in childhood. In 1990, the Williams family moved from Compton, California to Florida so Serena and Venus could receive professional training. Serena played her first professional event at age fourteen.

"You really have to learn to accept who you are and love who you are. I'm really happy with my body type, and I'm really proud of it."

The Williams sisters went on to become world-famous for their unparalleled prowess in a sport that historically has been hostile toward black athletes, and their singular talents have redefined the game. By the turn of the century, Serena and Venus were gracing the covers of sports magazines with broad smiles and beaded box braids emblematic of black culture in the 1990s. Serena has been forced to endure an endless barrage of misogynistic and racist body shaming for her muscular physique, dark skin, and natural hair. Despite this unwarranted hatred, Serena has become a strong role model for black women and girls globally.

Throughout her career, Serena has leveraged her platform to elevate issues of injustice. In 2008, she founded the Serena Williams Foundation to support young people affected by violence and to fund educational opportunities for children around the world. In 2011, she was appointed as a UNICEF goodwill ambassador focusing on global education and maternal health. In 2016, she and Venus established the Williams Sisters Fund to team up on philanthropic efforts with the same tenacity the two show on the tennis court.

Serena's tennis career has spanned decades, and her unwavering upward trajectory can be tracked through the timeline of her accomplishments: In 1999, she won her first major championship, the US Open singles title. In 2002 and 2003, for the first time, she won four Grand Slam titles in a row—the French Open, Wimbledon, the US Open, and the Australian Open. In January 2017, while she was two months pregnant, Serena secured her twenty-third Grand Slam at the Australian Open. With twenty-three Grand Slam singles titles and four Olympic gold medals, Serena Williams is the reigning queen of tennis and is considered by many to be the greatest athlete of all time.

SOLANGE KNOWLES

so-LAHNJ NOHLZ

Solange Knowles was born on June 24, 1986, in Houston, Texas. At the age of thirteen, Solange joined her older sister, **Beyoncé**, on tour with her all-women music group Destiny's Child. The group was a family business, managed by their father and with costumes designed by their mother, **Tina Knowles**. Starting as a backup dancer for the group, Solange made her official debut as a singer on the Destiny's Child album *8 Days of Christmas*. At sixteen, she released *Solo Star*, her first album, and soon spread her wings both as an actor and as a songwriter for her sister and for singer **Kelly Rowland**.

In 2007, Solange released her second album, *Sol-Angel and the Hadley St. Dreams*, and began to publicly celebrate her black heritage. As she worked on her third album, *True*, she began wearing a natural afro hairstyle and faced racist criticism from media outlets. While disapproving statements from fashion commentators and pop culture outlets calling hair "unruly" and "unkempt" proliferated, Solange continued to focus on her work. In 2013, she launched her own record label, Saint Records. The same year, drawing on inspiration from poet **Gil-Scott Heron**, Saint Records presented *Saint Heron*, a collaborative compilation album featuring eleven independent artists. Today, Saint Heron is an innovative online platform run by Solange and a team of black creatives and content creators where artists and activists share their unique stories.

Solange's singular sound and dedication to diverse black representation are reminiscent of the Motown and jazz-funk artists from whom she draws inspiration. In 2015, she became increasingly vocal about her support of the Black Lives Matter movement and released "Rise," a single that addressed the protests against **police violence** in Ferguson, Missouri, and Baltimore, Maryland. In 2016, Solange took to the streets and attended a peaceful youth-led rally organized by **Myra Richardson** in Baton Rouge, Louisiana, where many activists were arrested. Months later, "Rise" became the lead track on her breakthrough album, *A Seat at the Table*, where she unapologetically addressed a variety of injustices and **microaggressions** facing the black community. *A Seat at the Table* reached number one on the Billboard chart and led to Solange's first Grammy win in 2017.

Today, Solange is a musical and visual artist, model, fashion icon, and activist against injustice.

> "As far back as I can remember, our mother always taught us to be in control of our voice and our bodies and our work, and she showed us that through her example."

MASTERING
MODERN MEDIA

———————

The advent of the internet age and the subsequent dot-com boom drastically changed how people communicate and access information. Personal computers, web browsers, and search engines brought the internet to everyday people and allowed folks outside of the tech industry to surf the Web. In 1995, only 14 percent of American adults had internet access compared with 88.5 percent in 2016. Considering all of human history, these technological advancements took place in an incredibly short time. The social networking website Facebook was founded in 2004, and in 2016 it was used by two out of every seven people on the planet. In 2005, the video-sharing platform YouTube came into existence and in 2018 it was used to view almost five billion videos every day. In 2006, Twitter, the microblogging and social networking site responsible for the hashtag, was founded, and is now used by millions of people around the world, including innumerable **grassroots** activists who use it to circumvent the censorship of governments and institutions. All of these platforms became instantly accessible with the rise of smartphones. The collision of the Internet, social sharing platforms, and technological innovations continues to tear down the boundaries of traditional— and exclusionary—media.

But along with the benefits and advancements offered by these platforms come new threats and challenges. Unsurprisingly, the prejudices and biases of the offline world carry over to the online realm, and social platforms can be hotbeds of **harassment** and hate speech. As a result, tech companies often struggle to ensure the privacy and safety of their users, and they have not always done a great job of addressing hate speech. Social sharing platforms—and many would say the world at large—benefit immensely from the contributions made by the vibrant landscape of people of color, women, **queer**, **nonbinary**, and disabled folks.

Along with the cultural shift brought about by new media came language like "going viral," "hashtag," "influencer," and "troll" to explain the elements of the phenomenon. Those in the fields of entertainment, fashion, and journalism were quick to enter the new media arena. Political campaigns, like that of President **Barack Obama**, leveraged the organizing power of young people who were taking to these new entities to make their voices heard, showing how powerful these platforms can be. As traditional media industries and institutions attempted to stake out space in the digital landscape, a new generation of storytellers began to shape their own stories, produce their own content, and master their own opportunities with limited censorship from the people in power.

In "Mastering Modern Media," we will learn about individuals who are taking advantage of new technology to make previously unseen and unheard stories known.

ADITI JUNEJA

ah-DEE-tee joo-NAY-jah

Aditi Juneja was born on November 26, 1990, in Chandigarh, India. In 1991, Aditi and her family moved to the United States when her mother was offered a position at Rockefeller University. At the age of ten, Aditi was diagnosed with epilepsy, a neurological condition that causes seizures. That same year, she became a naturalized citizen of the United States. These intersecting experiences from her childhood would foreshadow her work in activism as an adult.

Early on, Aditi learned about American history through the eyes of her parents, who believed in a romanticized vision of their new home. She never believed that America was perfect, but she was encouraged by the idea of a democratic system that allows ordinary citizens to participate in governance. With her understanding of the US government and encouragement from her family, Aditi came to believe that she could have a direct role in making the reality of America more like the place her parents envisioned.

Armed with this belief, Aditi earned a degree in economics from Connecticut College in 2012 and a law degree from New York University in 2017. Following the 2016 election of President Donald Trump, Aditi began to use her legal scholarship to curate a centralized place for others to get involved. In collaboration with the nonprofit organization Stay Woke, she cocreated the Resistance Manual, a crowdsourced, free, and accessible online platform where all people can learn about policy, process, and ways to get involved at the federal and state levels. Creating the Resistance Manual allowed Aditi to leverage her legal education to make a concrete contribution to the movement known as The Resistance by creating a resource that explained the complex network that comprises American politics. Aditi's experience as a person with a disability made her thoughtful in how she pursued activism. Everything from the Resistance Manual's reading level, to the time commitment asked of volunteers, to the location and physical accessibility of events are inclusive.

Today, Aditi is a writer, lawyer, and disability justice advocate bringing accessibility to the forefront of movement building. Her work builds upon the legacy of a disability justice advocates, like Alice Wong.

> "I do not believe I need to be fixed, because I am not broken. The world may create barriers to my full participation sometimes, but I am a whole person."

AMANDLA STENBERG

uh-MAND-lah STEN-berg

Amandla Stenberg was born on October 23, 1998, in Los Angeles, California. In 2010, Amandla broke into the film industry in the action movie *Colombiana*. The *New York Times* applauded the young actor's skills as demonstrating an innate ability to capture the hearts of viewers worldwide. Amandla also became widely known for the role of Rue in the hugely successful film adaptation of *The Hunger Games*, for which she was nominated for an NAACP Image Award and won a Teen Choice Award.

In 2015, Amandla shared an online video essay entitled "Don't Cash Crop My Cornrows." In under five minutes, the then-sixteen-year-old explained cultural appropriation—the phenomenon of valuing elements of a minority group's culture only when they are adopted by members of a dominant group—in addition to a brief history of black hair culture and the practicality of hairstyles deemed undesirable by mainstream media. Using her platform, Amandla brought the important conversation about cultural appropriation to the wider public. The same year, Amandla released *Niobe: She Is Life*, a graphic novel about a black warrior. In interviews Amandla emphasized that *Niobe* features a lead character that shatters conventions of traditional heroes.

In 2016, Amandla continued to defy traditional parameters of celebrity and influence by disrupting mainstream conversations about gender through a personal story. Amandla revealed that she uses she/her as well as they/them pronouns, introducing the conversation about pronoun usage and nonbinary gender identity to a new audience. After revealing her nonbinary and bisexual identity on Tumblr, Amandla took the conversation to media outlets where she explained her disagreement with present conversations about gender identity. In 2017, 20 percent of millennials indicated that they identify as a gender nonbinary, meaning that they do not identify within the traditional gender binary of "woman/man." While Amandla is not the first public figure to identify as nonbinary, her public declaration of self provided a frame of reference for a new generation.

Today, Amandla is known for her acting prowess and advocacy work within the fields of racial justice and LGBTQ rights. Amandla's talents across a variety of mediums have enabled her multimedia approach to activism, and she communicates her messages not just as a highly celebrated and visible nonbinary actor, but through self-produced videos and a willingness to share personal experiences with a wide audience.

FEMINISTA JONES

feh-muh-NEE-stah JONES

Feminista Jones is a mental health social worker, sex-positive feminist writer, public speaker, and community activist. She was born in 1979 in Queens, New York, and grew up in the Bronx.

After earning her undergraduate degree at the University of Pennsylvania, Feminista went on to study social work at Hunter College in New York City. She grew up in similar conditions to those of the people she works with and advocates for, and since childhood has wanted to do her part to make life better for those who lack access to the resources they need to succeed and achieve their dreams. She is also a mother, a mentor to girls and women, and an outspoken advocate for people living in poverty and experiencing homelessness, and those living with psychiatric disabilities.

In 2013, Feminista published a now-iconic essay in *Salon* titled, "Is Twitter the underground railroad of activism?" In the piece, she voiced her view on the importance of social media in grassroots mobilization and protest, and revealed the historical context of the online community known as Black Twitter. According to Feminista, Black Twitter follows the legacy of African American spirituals and hip-hop, and is used by the black community to subvert and survive within systems of oppression.

As a notable voice of Black Twitter, Feminista uses her dynamic social media influence to shed light on sexual abuse, interpersonal violence, harassment, and more. In 2014, she launched a global anti-harassment campaign, #YouOKSis. The hashtag focused on black women because they are disproportionately likely to experience violence and harassment. In 2014, black women were murdered at a rate more than twice as high as that of white women, making the need for #YouOKSis demonstrable.

Also in 2014, Feminista created the National Moment of Silence, which gathered over a hundred thousand people across five countries to stand in solidarity against police violence. In 2015, she became the cofounder and general director of the Women's Freedom Conference, the first all-digital, free online conference created, developed, and presented solely by women of color.

Feminista is an award-winning blogger and author of the acclaimed novel, *Push the Button*. She has presented and lectured at various conferences and universities on feminism, black liberation, rape culture, and digital media organizing. Today, Feminista continues to use grassroots and digital organizing tactics to bring awareness about issues of gender-based violence, gun violence, and anti-black racism.

FRANCHESCA RAMSEY

fran-CHESS-kah RAM-zee

Franchesca Ramsey was born on November 29, 1983, and was raised in West Palm Beach, Florida. As a child, Franchesca's teachers frequently asked her to focus and stop talking so much. She was always quick with something clever and witty to say. When her kindergarten threatened to talk to Franchesca's mother if she didn't stop talking in class, Franchesca retorted, "That's okay, she'll still love me."

> "Make sure you listen and be willing to admit when you're wrong and be willing to learn. You're never going to be perfect. Everyone makes mistakes because we're human. But being open to being corrected and working to better yourself is the best and first thing everybody should be working toward."

As an adult, Franchesca's talent for talking became an asset. After studying graphic design at Miami International University and acting at the University of Michigan, she started a career as a graphic designer and soon began performing stand-up comedy and making YouTube videos. Franchesca yearned for her break into the entertainment industry so she could pursue a career in writing and comedy, but discrimination and gatekeeping kept her—and countless other black women and women of color—away from a big break. So, in 2012, she facilitated her own entry into the industry by using digital media to combine her comedic prowess and knack for social commentary in a YouTube video called "Shit White Girls Say . . . to Black Girls." When the video went viral, Franchesca's YouTube channel had a modest ten-thousand subscribers. Within five days of posting, her video had received over five million views. While Franchesca did not intend to become an activist, she had captivated a massive audience hungry for her raw approach to explaining **microaggressions**. Seizing upon the success, Franchesca used her new visibility to secure an acting agent and break into the business. Her meteoric rise to prominence is detailed in her book, *Well, That Escalated Quickly*, which has been applauded by industry leaders like **Luvvie Ajayi** and **Issa Rae**.

Since her ascent to fame, Franchesca and her original YouTube videos have been featured on MTV, BBC, MSNBC, and *Anderson Live*, and in 2016, she became a writer and contributor on *The Nightly Show with Larry Wilmore*. Today Franchesca captivates audiences on screen and as a writer, using comedy to educate millions of viewers about social injustice at the intersections of race and **gender**.

ISSA RAE

EES-uh RAY

Issa Rae was born Jo-Issa Rae Diop, on January 12, 1985. From a young age, Issa was fascinated with the stories of her diverse heritage—her mother is originally from Louisiana, while her father is from Senegal. Her childhood years were split between Los Angeles and Dakar, Senegal. She discovered her love of storytelling and acting in high school in Los Angeles, and was in college when Facebook and YouTube became staples of American young adulthood. These tools allowed Issa to share her original content with a wider audience. While studying at Stanford University, Issa spent her free time creating music videos, acting, and directing. She graduated from Stanford in 2007 with a bachelor's degree in African and African American studies and continued developing her storytelling skills in classes at the New York Film Academy.

Feeling that diverse portrayals of the black experience were severely lacking, she debuted her third web series *The Misadventures of Awkward Black Girl* in 2011. Hosted on YouTube, the series quickly grew a cult following, as it used humor to examine relatable and awkward encounters experienced by the main character, who was played by Issa. In 2012, the series received a Shorty Award for Best Web Series. When the series concluded after two seasons, Issa leveraged its success to launch a career in television as an actor, producer, and writer.

In 2015, Issa released her first book, *The Misadventures of Awkward Black Girl*, named after her hit web series. The book, which examined Issa's own story of self-acceptance, was widely praised and made the *New York Times* best seller list. The success of her web series and book led Issa to create the HBO comedy series *Insecure*, which debuted in 2016 to enormous critical acclaim. Loosely based on her web series and personal life, *Insecure* presents an honest window into the most intimate and uncomfortable experiences of black young adulthood, which have largely been missing from mainstream entertainment and media.

In addition to using her art to represent the realities of black experience, Issa has used her growing platform to address the police violence and injustice faced by the black community. Following the 2016 killing of Alton Sterling at the hands of police, Issa raised over $700,000 on behalf of the Sterling Family Trust. All of the funds raised went toward a college scholarship fund for Sterling's surviving children.

Today, Issa Rae continues to be recognized as an author, humanitarian, and important content creator who is flipping the script on media representation.

JACKIE AINA

JACK-ee EYE-nah

Jackie Aina was born on August 4, 1987, and grew up in La Puente, California. With a father from Nigeria and a mother from the United States, Jackie's childhood was shaped by an array of black cultural traditions. However, as a child, Jackie often struggled to be her vibrant and vocal self. Every action she took—like speaking up in class—was measured against the expectations society placed on her as a black girl. Despite these harmful perceptions, Jackie drew upon the legacy of African diasporic heritage to understand that the way the world treated her had no bearing on her personal worth.

Jackie began using makeup to express herself and quickly learned that her passion could become a career. After becoming licensed in cosmetology, Jackie began working with major cosmetic brands as a makeup artist. But as she entered the beauty industry, Jackie realized that the makeup options for people with dark complexions were few and far between. Like our society, the makeup industry participates in colorism, discrimination against individuals with dark skin tones and prioritization of individuals with light skin and Eurocentric features. In 2009, Jackie took to YouTube to show black women and women of color how to navigate the beauty industry and to encourage a larger community of budding beauty gurus to embrace their own definitions of beauty instead of the exclusionary ones imposed by society.

By 2012, Jackie was making waves in the beauty community for calling out the lack of foundation shades, lip colors, and skin care options for dark-skinned individuals. In 2016, she took her discussions about colorism to a new level with a series of educational videos that specifically debunked the numerous lies based in racism and colorism that society asserts about people with dark skin. Her videos cover a variety of important subjects including colorism, light skin privilege, internalized racism, and more, bringing these issues to the attention of a wide and diverse audience.

Jackie's influence has been far-reaching, and while she is known for calling beauty brands to account for perpetuating colorism, she also moves forward with brands that seek to be part of the solution. In 2017, Jackie announced a collaboration with the makeup line Too Faced to make the brand's line of Born This Way foundations more inclusive for dark-skinned folks. In 2018, she became the first ever recipient of the NAACP Image Awards' YouTuber of the Year award for her dedication to ending colorism and bias within the beauty industry and society at large.

KAT BLAQUE

CAT BLACK

Kat Blaque was born on September 14, 1990, in Lynwood, California. As a child, Kat had a knack for creative expression and loved to paint, draw, and make crafts. Early on, her teachers and parents encouraged her artistic talents, and in fifth grade, her mother took her to an animation expo for youth of color where she was first exposed to the possibility of a career as a creative.

In middle school, Kat struggled with depression and negative body image, but theater and drama classes helped her gain confidence in herself and her voice. At the time, she had been blogging on a (now defunct) platform, Xanga. Through conversations with her readers and community on Xanga, she began to realize that she might be genderqueer, a term that for her meant that she was simultaneously all genders and no gender.

As a young adult, Kat went to study at the California Institute of the Arts, where she realized her transgender identity. Though her decision to transition into womanhood was an impediment to finishing her education, Kat began making creative works about her transition. She used her YouTube channel to document and discuss her experiences with taking hormones and anti-androgens she had to purchase from dubious online pharmacies without a prescription. Through videos and blog posts, Kat showcased the reality of life and challenges of health care access for many people within the transgender community. As a result, Kat's digital media became a source of education for people of all genders searching for answers about gender identity and expression. By her last year of art school, she had legally changed her name and, for a while, chose to be "stealth," hiding her transgender identity for her safety. Despite the potential risks, Kat gradually became more passionate about being visible as a transgender person in new media, and decided to be open about her transition.

As Janet Mock has said, Kat is a "prolific trans YouTuber." By openly showing so much of her life and transition, she has inspired many LGBTQ young people and helped educate the public at large about LGBTQ issues.

"Don't make it about you, don't recenter the conversation about you. Your job as an ally is to uplift the voice of who you are supporting. It's not healthy to speak for us, there are so many trans people who want to speak for themselves. People may give you way more validity, so the best thing to do as an ally is to let them speak."

MICHELLE PHAN

mih-SHELL FAH-ng

Michelle Phan was born on April 11, 1987, as one of ten siblings in a large Vietnamese American family. At age fourteen, Michelle's mother escaped Vietnam as a war refugee, and Michelle grew up intimately aware of the ways she benefitted from her mother's determination. During her teen years, Michelle struggled to carve out a path that both honored her Vietnamese heritage and allowed her to define her own identity. She resolved to focus on her creative talents and enrolled in the Ringling College of Art and Design.

In college, Michelle experimented with different forms of creative expression like painting and graphic design. When she started to use her face as a canvas, she realized that makeup enabled her to express a unique and multifaceted identity. In 2005, she began sharing her makeup tips and knowledge on her blog on the (now defunct) platform Xanga, and soon her audience of readers began asking for video tutorials. In 2007, Michelle posted her first makeup tutorial to YouTube, which earned over forty thousand views in just a few hours. Since this initial tutorial, she has become a YouTube phenomenon and influencer, continuing to post about her life, beauty secrets, and favorite products to an audience of millions. Michelle's successes as a woman of color in the predominantly white beauty industry speak to the way that digital media platforms like YouTube have empowered a new generation of diverse storytellers.

In 2011, Michelle transformed the platform she had developed since college into a business model and cofounded ipsy, an online beauty community and subscription service. Michelle also launched ipsy Open Studios, a content creation studio which provided the technology and editing equipment necessary to excel in the digital media landscape. Through these initiatives, Michelle broke ground as a woman of color, digital native, and entrepreneur. In 2013, Michelle partnered with L'Oreal to launch her very own makeup line, em cosmetics. She honored her Vietnamese heritage by dedicating the brand to her mother and naming the cosmetic line "em," which is a Vietnamese word expressing youth, and a term of endearment and adoration. The following year, Michelle released her first book, *Make Up: Your Life Guide to Beauty, Style, and Success—Online and Off*, providing readers with a primer on how to take one's own unique talents and transform them into a path of entrepreneurship and brand development. Michelle Phan is an award-winning and trailblazing content creator who has touched the lives of millions by mastering modern media.

MONA HAYDAR

MOE-nah HAY-dar

Rapper, poet, and **feminist** Mona Haydar was born on May 18, 1988, into a large Syrian American family in Flint, Michigan. Growing up with seven siblings taught Mona about the importance of collaboration—when her family ate foods that required a lot of labor, such as rolled grape leaves, her mother would say, "You don't roll, you don't eat," to teach her kids the importance of pitching in.

Mona started penning poetry as soon as she was old enough to write. One of her first poems in a kindergarten journal went: "I am mood. I am dude. I am Mona." And from the age of thirteen, Mona has been doing spoken word and performance poetry. Though she had been using the written word to chronicle important moments in her life, in 2017 Mona revealed herself to be a skilled rapper with the debut of her hit single, "Hijabi." Through the lyrics, Mona uplifts Muslim women around the world who choose to wear **hijab**. In the music video, she is seen eight months pregnant with her second son, disrupting the socially accepted idea of what a woman should look like in a music video. Within days of its release, the single earned over a million views on YouTube and another million on Facebook and Mona emerged as a visible feminist Muslim woman dedicated to uplifting all women in the face of hatred and **sexism**. "Hijabi" represents Mona's approach to music: her lyrics challenge stereotypes about Muslim women and investigate the supremacy of **patriarchy** within Arab culture and faith traditions.

Like **Missy Elliott** and countless women MCs before her, Mona has carved out a place for her in the music industry as a woman rapper. She uses music to combine her feminist and religious scholarship with her natural talent for the written and spoken word to create music that resonates across cultural and religious identity. Mona continues to break the stereotypes typically assigned to Muslim women, and shatters the boundaries of the music industry by being a woman addressing spiritual topics in a male-centered and secular industry.

> "Acts of violence make it all the more obvious that those of us who believe in love need to work even harder to counter hate and violence to manifest our more beautiful world."

TAYE HANSBERRY

TAY HANZ-berry

Taye Hansberry was born in Los Angeles, California. Raised by a single mother and a brigade of bold matriarchs, women's empowerment became an integral part of Taye's development. As the grandniece of Lorraine Hansberry, storytelling also became a passion of Taye's as she learned about the work her grandaunt had accomplished as a playwright.

As an adult Taye became a self-taught photographer, and once she picked up a camera, she never put it down. After earning a degree in communications at UC Santa Barbara, Taye enrolled in classes at Santa Barbara City College to hone her technical editing skills. Despite her extensive photography portfolio, Taye struggled as a woman photographer in a largely male field, and while she could not get an apprenticeship with an established photographer, she was determined to get her work out into the world. In 2010 Taye started a blog called *Stuff She Likes* as a way to promote her photography. The launch of her blog coincided with the debut of the visual media and social sharing application, Instagram. The name of her blog capitalized on the new phenomenon of "liking" posts and images to demonstrate admiration on social media. After four years of incremental growth, the blog took off in 2014, and Taye began earning invitations to exclusive events, brand ambassadorships, music festivals, and on-air media spots. Since then, she has been featured in publications such as *Vogue*, *Glamour*, *Vanity Fair*, and *Who What Wear* in addition to hosting fashion segments on nationally syndicated morning shows.

As her popularity grew, Taye did not shy away from bringing her family's Creole heritage to the forefront of her work. Many of Taye's blog entries and social media posts educate her followers about the food, music, and traditions that her family celebrates. Through her work, she also pays homage to her grandaunt Lorraine Hansberry, and has helped to elevate the playwright's legacy into pop culture consciousness.

Throughout her career, Taye has worked to break down the silos that fashion and beauty industries place individuals into. In 2013, she used her blog to shut down the notion that race must determine one's hair texture, bringing forward a more nuanced discussion of race, beauty, and identity.

Through her platform, Taye routinely addresses society's biases, whether she is writing about New York's Fashion Week, travel, or her own life experiences. Taye also mentors other content creators and strongly believes in building up new media titans as she enjoys the successes of her impactful work.

VILISSA THOMPSON

vuh-LISS-ah TOMP-sun

Vilissa Thompson was born on September 17, 1985, in Columbia, South Carolina. Vilissa is a social worker, educator, and a prominent leader promoting self-advocacy and empowerment among people with disabilities, especially black disabled women.

During fetal development, Vilissa was diagnosed with osteogenesis imperfecta, better known as brittle bone disease, which affects her bone development and height. Around the age of five, Vilissa got her first wheelchair, and at thirteen, she was diagnosed as hard of hearing. Growing up with a disability, Vilissa saw very few disabled black women in the media, which made her feel erased by society. Feeling invisible inspired Vilissa to be the representation she needed to see in the world and become the role model she wished she had. For Vilissa, being an advocate has afforded her the opportunity to share her life experiences as a black disabled woman, and to provide an image and example for other women like her.

After graduating in 2008 from Winthrop University with a bachelor's of arts in psychology and a minor in African American studies, Vilissa returned to school for her master's in social work in 2012. While starting her a career as a social worker, Vilissa launched Ramp Your Voice!, an organization and website that discusses the disability experience from an intersectional lens, in 2013.

As conversations about diversity spread online in 2016, Vilissa called the disability community to account with the creation of the viral hashtag #DisabilityTooWhite. This online campaign shed light on the lack of diversity within the disability community and the way this lack of representation prevents disabled people of color from feeling validated and accepted. Vilissa's work is an important departure from the notion that activism facilitated through social media is somehow a lesser form of advocacy. For Vilissa, social media sites and personal blogs are tools for resistance. To further educate allies and community members alike, Vilissa launched "Black Disabled Woman Syllabus," a compilation of books, essays, articles, speeches, and music, which accurately explain the diversity within black identity and the nuanced experience of black disabled women.

Through education and the use of digital tools, Vilissa continues her commitment to making the visibility of diverse disabled experiences a permanent reality. Vilissa draws upon the support of her community to continue getting into "good trouble" and creating the change she hopes to see in the world.

POWER TO THE PEOPLE

DISABILITY RIGHTS ARE HUMAN RIGHTS

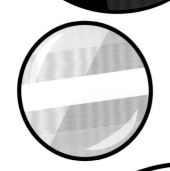

STUDENT POWER

END WHITE SILENCE

NO JUSTICE NO PEACE

THE REVOLUTION WILL BE OURS

———

I f a revolution aims to liberate those facing oppression and hardship, it must be inclusive of *everyone* facing oppression and hardship—not just the largest or most dominant groups among the oppressed.

In Chapter 1, we learned about historic and symbolic erasure through the stories of **Sylvia Rivera** and **Marsha P. Johnson**. While these **transgender** women of color led the new era of **LGBTQ** organizing, contemporary movements attempted to shut them out of the very initiatives they created. As Sylvia fought for incarcerated LGBTQ people and those experiencing homelessness, members of the LGBTQ community with more access repeatedly moved to silence her. Nevertheless, she persisted. Just as Sylvia and Marsha refused to be removed from history, today's social justice organizers continue to carve out a place for themselves and their communities in current movements. This generation of revolutionaries refuses to be silenced.

During the 2017 **Women's March**, activist and writer **Raquel Willis** vocalized the failures of women's rights movements in her moving speech "A Vision of Liberation." Raquel described a vibrant and possible future of fair and equal treatment for everyone. She challenged the audience to bring forth "a world where our Native family isn't silenced on land that was stolen from them. A world where transgender kids don't wake up and go to schools where the teachers and staff are indistinguishable from bullies. A world where a black person isn't struck down by law enforcement. A world where **sex workers** aren't demonized and cast away. A world where brave immigrants aren't vilified for moving for a better life. A world where black and brown transgender women don't have their lives taken just for existing. A world where people with disabilities are fully counted and represented. A world where women have the right to choose the fate of their bodies."

The figures of *Modern HERstory* have fought—and are still fighting—to realize this future. Everyday people are rejecting a feminism that only fights for white straight **cisgender** able-bodied women. Instead, they are declaring, "The revolution will be ours," that it will be for all of us, not just some of us. It will include people like me, and people like Raquel, and advocates like Marsha P. Johnson. Whether you and I come from the same background, speak the same language, face the same obstacles—or not—you are a part of the future we are building together.

As our broader society remains entrenched in archaic ideology and refuses to acknowledge these necessary advancements, organizers are continuing to move forward for the collective liberation of all people. "The Revolution Will Be Ours" is dedicated to nine organizers and firebrand revolutionaries who are disrupting convention and social expectations to forge an inclusive and equitable future for all of us—no matter what.

DR. ADRIENNE KEENE

AY-dree-en KEEN

Dr. Adrienne Keene of the Cherokee Nation was born on October 20, 1985, in Encinitas, California. When she was in fifth grade, her class was studying Native Americans and had a homework assignment to make up an "Indian name" by combining an adjective with an animal or other nature-related noun. Adrienne discussed the assignment with her mother, and together they decided that Adrienne would use her grandmother's name, Mona Mae. In class the next day, her classmates offered names and explanations like, "'Running Bear,' because I run fast and am strong like a bear." When Adrienne shared her "Indian" name, her classmates snickered, but she was proud that she took a stand for her Cherokee heritage and against Native American stereotypes.

Working to end the stereotyping and erasure of Native communities in the United States continued to be an interest of Adrienne's as she grew up. Throughout her life she saw cultural appropriation—such as music festival attendees wearing indigenous headdresses as costumes—and learned about the educational disparities experienced in Native communities. After earning degrees in cultural and social anthropology and Native studies at Stanford, she began to realize the lack of research on the needs of Native students. Working to resolve this gap, she went to Harvard for her doctorate in education, focusing her research on college access for Native students. She then did a post-doctoral fellowship in Native American studies at Brown University, and began teaching American studies and ethnic studies.

Adrienne continued to be concerned by the systemic misrepresentation of Native Americans in mainstream culture. Out of these feelings of frustration and invisibility she started the blog Native Appropriations, where she writes about cultural appropriation and stereotypes of Native peoples in fashion, film, music, and other forms of pop culture. In 2014 she also launched Natives Against Redsk*ns an online petition for American Indian, Alaska Native, Native Hawaiian, First Nations, and other Indigenous Peoples who believe that the name of the Washington, D.C., football team is offensive and needs to change. Through this and a myriad of other initiatives, Dr. Adrienne Keene has rallied a community of activists and allies to work for the visibility, voices, and rights of Native Americans.

Today, Adrienne continues her work as an activist, writer, and organizer of the *Native Appropriations* community. The website and online community have added and amplified Native voices to the ongoing conversations around cultural appropriation of Native American culture and customs.

ALENCIA JOHNSON

ah-LEN-see-ah JON-sun

Alencia Johnson was born on September 3, 1987, and grew up in Fredericksburg, Virginia, with a deep connection to the Christian faith community. Alencia's parents, who were both leaders in their church, taught her about Jesus Christ as a radical activist who fought for the most marginalized individuals within society. Alencia's faith became a central part of her identity and inspired a lifelong commitment to advocacy and her belief that humanity exists to live in service to others.

> "Nobody else is telling me what I can and cannot do with my body, and that is liberating beyond any means."

While attending Christopher Newport University, Alencia organized students to take action on important social issues and joined the historic African American sorority Delta Sigma Theta. As president of the university's Multicultural Student Association, she organized several anti-racism protests on campus. In an era before #BlackLivesMatter and widespread use of social media, Alencia learned to organize communities and elevate nuanced conversations about race with limited resources. In 2009, Alencia graduated with a degree in communications and leadership studies.

In 2012, she took her skills as a communication professional and her passion for social change to Chicago to work on President Barack Obama's reelection campaign, for which she developed and implemented media strategies for urban television and radio. After President Obama won the 2012 election, Alencia joined the team at Planned Parenthood as a press officer focusing on communication strategies for the black community. As her work progressed, she identified a need for a dedicated team to address the unique health care needs of underserved communities. Three years later, she became the organization's first Director of Constituency Communications, a completely new department focusing on faith communities, LGBTQ communities, communities of color, and young people.

Today, Alencia continues to blaze new trails in the world of health care access and social justice. She is a mentor, educator, and strategist recognized for her commitment to justice and virtue.

ANJALI PARAY

ahn-ja-LEE paa-RAY

Born on May 19, 1979 in Brooklyn, New York, Anjali Paray's childhood was informed by the rich culture of her Guyanese and Indian parents, who made sure that a commitment to family, faith, and her cultural traditions were a central part of her upbringing. As a Hindu, Anjali was expected to attend temple up to three times a week where services were held in Hindi, and by age nine, she could sing in both English and Hindi. When she first started singing, her grandmother taught Anjali the fundamentals of music. But her grandmother only sang in a religious context, whereas Anjali found joy and meaning in secular music, too. Recognizing Anjali's musical inclinations, her parents promptly enrolled her in Indian classical music courses.

Early on, Anjali began writing songs herself, drawing influences for her music from both her home of New York and her international family heritage. She began using her music to bring her worlds together, creating a unique mix of classical and hip-hop sounds. To improve her skill, Anjali studied with composers and musicians across India and the United States, becoming an accomplished and deeply passionate musician during her early twenties.

At the age of twenty-two, having completed classical training and possessing a unique sound that mixes soul, R&B, and Indian classical music, Anjali was poised to break into the music industry. However, the tide of xenophobia and discrimination against individuals who were perceived to be Muslim in the wake of the terrorist attacks on September 11, 2001 thwarted Anjali's career. She is part of a group of unheard and unseen people who have been denied access to opportunities—and ultimately critical successes—due to discrimination. While mainstream labels and music bookers denied her entry into the field she loved, Anjali drew on the powerful memory of her grandmother and never gave up on her passion for music. She was compelled to make music that could help heal her Guyanese people, who currently hold one of the world's highest suicide rates, and to bring a voice to those stories many might not know about.

In 2018, Anjali Paray rereleased her first album, *Sacred Offerings*, and her sophomore album, *Big Human*, which had been in the making since 2011. While the tide of xenophobia is still palpable across the world, Anjali refuses to give up her passion for music and works to make her voice heard.

JENNICET GUTIÉRREZ

JEN-ee-set goo-tee-AIR-ez

Jennicet Gutiérrez was born on June 8, 1986, in Tuxpan, Jalisco, Mexico. Going against the expectations of society, she fought to express herself in the midst of bullying and harassment, identifying as transgender as early as six years old and transitioning at the age of twenty-seven. As a teen, she moved to the United States with her family from their hometown in Mexico. Jennicet learned English while attending high school in the United States and experienced the hardships and vulnerability of being an undocumented immigrant and having to constantly advocate for herself.

Throughout her adulthood, Jennicet has participated in community organizing efforts focusing on the LGBTQ and undocumented immigrant community. In 2014, she became a founding member of Familia: Trans Queer Liberation Movement, the first national organization in the United States to organize and advocate for LGBTQ Latinx people. Working with Familia, Jennicet continued supporting transgender women detained for their immigration status.

On June 24, 2015, Jennicet joined President Barack Obama and a host of LGBTQ advocates for the White House LGBTQ Pride reception. But unfortunately, the celebration did not reflect the reality she and her community were facing. As an undocumented and transgender activist, Jennicet took the opportunity to call attention to President Obama's callous treatment of undocumented immigrants and failure to address the brutalities faced by the trans community. In the midst of the jovial celebration, as President Obama concluded his speech, Jennicet interrupted him and exclaimed: "President Obama, release all LGBTQ [people] in detention centers. President Obama, stop the torture and abuse trans women face in detention centers. I'm tired of the violence we are facing. Not one more deportation. Ni una más deportación." Immediately, Jennicet was characterized as ungrateful and insolent for interrupting President Obama with a cry for justice. But she felt it was imperative to do her part in taking a stand with those in her community who are left behind as others are experiencing progress. Through her act of defiance, she set an important standard for contemporary movements to be fiercely inclusive.

Today, Jennicet's activist work aims to create a world where people do not have to live in fear, where people are uplifted and celebrated for who they are. By living as an open and proud transgender woman and immigrant, she is a role model and an icon.

LAYSHIA CLARENDON

LAY-shah CLAIR-en-dun

Layshia Clarendon was born on May 2, 1991, in San Bernardino, California. Athleticism, and basketball in particular, have been woven into the fabric of the Clarendon family identity since Layshia was young. Her father was a high school basketball referee for over a decade, and her older sister played basketball as well. It was inevitable that Layshia would become part of this family tradition. Despite Layshia's success on the court and in school, her sexual orientation became a controversial subject at home. Even after she earned a four-year basketball scholarship to a major university, her parents struggled to fully support their **queer** daughter and considered her identity to be a point of shame.

Layshia earned her bachelor's degree in American studies from UC Berkeley, where she was a star of the women's basketball program. In 2013 she led the Berkeley Women's basketball team to their first Final Four appearance in history. It was in college that Layshia became open about her sexual orientation—her truth as a queer woman mattered more than what anyone in the world thought.

After college, Layshia went pro, and started her WNBA career as a first-round draft pick for the Indiana Fever, playing with the team from 2013 to 2015. In 2016, Layshia was traded to the Atlanta Dream, where she was a starting point guard on the team.

On and off the court Layshia is a passionate leader and community advocate inspired by her Christian faith. Empowered by her faith to embrace her sexual orientation, Layshia realized her years of living **closeted** were preparing her for a larger purpose. With the platform earned from her athletic career, Layshia became emboldened to be a role model for **LGBTQ** youth by unapologetically being herself. Since her rookie WNBA season, Layshia has used her platform to be an outspoken advocate for the LGBTQ and black communities. She has spoken on numerous panels across the United States for organizations and outlets including the **Human Rights Campaign**, the *Sports Business Journal*, and the *Atlantic*. In advancing her activism, Layshia has partnered with **Athlete Ally**, a nonprofit organization dedicated to ending homophobia and transphobia in sports and to educating athletic communities to stand up against hate.

Today, Layshia hopes to promote inclusion in athletics, raise awareness around **intersectionality**, and bridge the divide between LGBTQ and faith communities.

LORI RODRIGUEZ

LOH-ree rod-REE-gezz

Lori Rodriguez was born on March 27, 1991, in Los Angeles, California, to immigrant parents from El Salvador and Guatemala. Lori's mother, a sweatshop worker in El Salvador, came to the United States in young adulthood and went on to create her own clothing line. Moving frequently following their parent's divorce and often being the new kid on the block, Lori witnessed firsthand the way society looks down on immigrants and low-income families. But they also saw how prejudice could also fade away through compassion and education.

Coming out as queer and exploring their non-binary gender identity within the chaos of frequent relocation, Lori looked forward to their family's road trips, which interrupted the complexities of life with the serenity of nature. When Lori first saw the Milky Way from the mountains of Yosemite at eleven years old, they were reassured by the idea of diverse celestial bodies coming together to make something beautiful. From that moment forward, Lori wanted to help others understand the value and importance of difference.

Lori graduated from Reed College in 2013 with a degree in religious studies. In order to stay close to nature and to begin working in education, Lori took a position at the Community Cycling Center, a nonprofit bike shop in Portland where they served as a curriculum development specialist and bike safety instructor. They also began to organize against gentrification, racism, and unfair labor practices in Portland and joined Basic Rights Oregon as a Communications Fellow.

In 2016, Lori moved to New York City in order to utilize their expertise as a communicator and organizer within the field of reproductive health. In Planned Parenthood's communications department, Lori began overseeing the Spanish translation efforts for the organization's Constituency Communications Department spearheaded by Alencia Johnson. During the rise of the Zika virus in the southern United States, Lori used their experience in education to adapt jargon-heavy materials about the virus into easy-to-understand flyers available in English, Spanish, and Haitian Creole. These documents measurably impacted the community's knowledge and preparedness about Zika virus.

In early 2017, Lori left Planned Parenthood to focus on the development of the resource hub at Equality for HER, a nonprofit educational platform founded by Blair Imani in 2014. As the startup's first ever Director of Research and Partnerships, Lori is part of a diverse team aiming to bring conversations about social justice to a wider audience.

RAQUEL WILLIS

rah-KELL WILL-iss

Raquel Willis was born on May 22, 1991, and raised in Augusta, Georgia. Raquel's parents brought her up in the Southern Black Christian tradition. From a young age, she was instilled with the values of service to the community and volunteering with the church, which inform her approach to activism today. Raquel has identified as gender-nonconforming since she was a child. However, it was not until high school that she decided to come out as queer. She saw coming out as a way to not only create a space for herself but to create spaces for others as well.

While studying communications at the University of Georgia, Raquel learned about feminism and gender theory. After college, Raquel worked as a news reporter in Monroe, Georgia, where she was forced to hide her transgender identity by being "stealth." Raquel struggled to work while having to hide her full self for over a year. Leaving her role as a news reporter and moving to Atlanta, Raquel began to use her knack for storytelling alongside grassroots organizers with the Solutions Not Punishments Coalition to end police profiling of transgender women of color and mass incarceration. Her work as a communicator and organizer caught the attention of the Transgender Law Center (TLC), where she began working after moving to Oakland, California, in 2015. TLC is the largest organization in the United States advocating on behalf of transgender and gender-nonconforming people. Starting as a Communications Associate, Raquel went on to become a national organizer with TLC, assisting and training transgender and gender-nonconforming activists and advocates across the country.

Raquel is also a speaker who has lectured across the nation on the current state of trans activism. In January 2017, she was a featured speaker at the Women's March on Washington, calling for the inclusion of transgender women of color in all movements. As a writer, Raquel is a part of Echoing Ida, a national black women's writing collective.

> "When you belittle and devalue trans women and their womanhood, you are operating as a tool of the patriarchy."

In addition to her grassroots efforts, Raquel is known for her voice on social media and unique analysis on identity, current events, and politics. She has the powerful ability to use social media and digital activism as tools of resistance and liberation. Today, she continues her work as an activist, mastering online and offline demonstrations and protests.

DR. SU'AD ABDUL KHABEER

sue-AHHD ab-DOOL kha-BEER

Dr. Su'ad Abdul Khabeer was born on June 10, 1978, in Syracuse, New York, and raised in Brooklyn. Su'ad's parents are converts to Islam and were each deeply involved in contemporary black liberation movements. Her father, an immigrant from Panama, came to the US in the 1960s. Her mother, a Harlem native with ancestry in Barbados and Montserrat, was a member of the Black Panther Party, and integrated her junior high school in Littleneck, New York, as a student activist.

Growing up in a community that blended the different elements of black heritage and Islamic tradition, she celebrated Kwanzaa, took African dance classes, and joined the Girl Scouts within her *masjid*, or house of worship. When the 1991 film *Daughters of the Dust* debuted, Su'ad's school took her and her classmates to see the movie. Elements of African tradition were prevalent throughout the film and one image that resonated with Su'ad was the depiction of a Muslim character who made *salat*—or began to pray—just as Su'ad did at home. Seeing this film was significant for Su'ad because it encompassed the many facets of her identity that she didn't often see represented in pop culture.

After completing her PhD in cultural anthropology from Princeton, graduating from the School of Foreign Service at Georgetown University, and completing the Islamic studies diploma program of the Institute at Abu Nour University in Damascus, Su'ad began to work at Purdue University in Indiana. Being immersed in this predominantly white community was very alienating, so she took to the online realm to create community. Together with fellow black Muslim women scholars, Su'ad began to build Sapelo Square, an online resource for the black Muslim community in the United States.

Sapelo Square launched on May 19, 2015, the ninetieth birthday of Malcolm X, to honor his legacy of advocacy and scholarship within the black Muslim community. *Sapelo Square* is named for an island off the coast of Georgia which housed one of the first communities of African Muslims in the United States in the early 1800s. It is the first website dedicated to the comprehensive documentation and analysis of the black American Muslim experience.

Today, Su'ad continues to focus on elevating the often erased and ignored elements of black Muslim identity and history. Through her 2016 book, *Muslim Cool: Race, Religion, and Hip Hop in the United States*, she examines the histories of Islam and hip-hop and how the intersecting ideas of Muslim and black identity transform discussions of race in the United States.

WINNIE HARLOW

WIN-nee HAR-low

Winnie Harlow was born Chantelle Brown-Young on July 27, 1994, in Toronto, Ontario. At the age of three, Winnie was diagnosed with vitiligo, a condition that causes depigmentation of the skin. Throughout her life, Winnie has been teased because of the patches of pale skin that contrast with her brown hues. While vitiligo is not dangerous or contagious, the social stigma associated with the skin condition can create an emotional burden for many individuals with the condition. In a 2017 interview with *Elle*, Winnie stated, "I think everyone naturally is really confident, but when you're deterred from believing you're perfect the way you are, that can lower your self-esteem."

Armed with the confidence of self, Winnie's unique image and body positive message quickly earned her recognition in the beauty and fashion industries. Winnie rose to prominence as a model when she was discovered on Instagram by Tyra Banks, supermodel and host of *America's Next Top Model*. In 2014, Winnie joined the reality competition show, where she advanced as a finalist. While Winnie did not win the competition, her appearance on the show made an indelible mark on the industry and provided a massive boost to her modeling career. Within two years of her TV appearance, Winnie was featured in many international fashion campaigns and became an inspiration for individuals across the globe to embrace their unique beauty.

In addition to modeling, Winnie has become an activist seeking to redefine conventional beauty standards. In 2014, after appearing on *America's Next Top Model*, she gave a speech at TEDxTeen titled, "My Story Is Painted on My Body," in which she encouraged people to celebrate the beauty within themselves. Winnie says, "The real difference isn't my skin. It's the fact that I don't find my beauty in the opinions of others." She is also an advocate of environmental conservation and has partnered with the beauty company Burt's Bees to spread awareness about the environmental impact of declining bee populations.

As a model and public-figure, Winnie Harlow has earned a reputation as a leader and innovator at the intersections of fashion and advocacy. Today, she continues to inspire others with her messages of self-love.

> "I think everyone naturally is really confident, but when you're deterred from believing you're perfect the way you are, that can lower your self-esteem."

THE REVOLUTION
WILL BE FUNDED

———

When women enter the world of business and bring forth their own companies and initiatives, it directly challenges the notion that only men can be legitimate and successful entrepreneurs and founders. In 2017, the US Department of Labor found that only 36 percent of all businesses are women-owned. Going against the traditional **patriarchy** in the world of business presents its own set of challenges, and oftentimes, women entrepreneurs face **harassment** and backlash. For this reason, the entry of women and **nonbinary** folks into this predominantly male field is an act of revolution in itself. By gaining the access and financial resources historically allowed only to men, women and nonbinary people are able to act as role models and enter into positions where wealth can be redistributed among communities outside of the status quo. Today, many people are using their access to resources facilitated by businesses and foundations to fund and further social change.

This has been borne out in many ways by the folks profiled in this chapter, like social justice entrepreneurs **Leslie Mac** and **Marissa Jenae Johnson,** founders of Safety Pin Box. In creating a monthly subscription box of educational tools for allies, they directly challenged the idea that black women must provide free labor for their own liberation. But since their service was built upon a framework of compensation, the launch of their revolutionary company was met with immediate backlash from those who seek to maintain white patriarchal control of wealth.

Amani Al-Khatahtbeh founded her groundbreaking media platform **Muslim Girl** to give Muslim women a mainstream outlet through which they could define their own experiences. While she has faced intense scrutiny and harassment online for allowing Muslim women to tell their own stories, her business continues to thrive. **Rihanna** has leveraged her immense global platform as a musician—and the kind of earnings that come with double platinum status—to become an advocate and philanthropist working to ensure that other girls can have opportunities, too.

In "The Revolution Will Be Funded," we will learn about ten individuals who are disrupting the current state of resource distribution through their commitments to sustaining movements, manufacturing ethical products, funding creators of change, and employing people from **marginalized groups** through their women-owned businesses.

AMANI AL-KHATAHTBEH

ah-MAN-ee al-kah-TOT-beh

Born on May 6, 1992, Palestinian and Jordanian American author, activist, and entrepreneur Amani Al-Khatahtbeh is the founder and editor in chief of Muslim Girl, the leading Muslim women's online publication. Growing up during a time of increased anti-Muslim rhetoric following the terrorist attacks on September 11, 2001, Amani struggled with bullying and harassment throughout her childhood and adolescence. The challenge of celebrating her identity while also trying to survive amidst the toxic rhetoric caused her to feel erased and silenced.

In 2009, while she was still in high school, Amani founded *Muslim Girl*. Like many marginalized groups, Muslim women are often forced to hear their stories from the mouths of others, especially in the mainstream media. *Muslim Girl* is an online platform designed to give voice to Muslim women and provide a space for them to tell their own stories in their own words. It has grown into a massive platform that curates personal stories and critical essays from contributors across the world and has been recognized for its groundbreaking work by *Teen Vogue*, *Forbes*, and many other notable institutions.

Inspired by the success of *Muslim Girl*, Amani wrote a memoir about her experience as a young Muslim woman born and raised in the United States.

In October 2016, just prior to the election of anti-Muslim President Donald Trump, Amani published *Muslim Girl: A Coming of Age*. The book helped give visibility to the experiences of Muslims in America during a time of heightened public intolerance. It has since been translated into many languages, allowing girls around the world to be inspired and empowered by Amani's story and journey.

Despite xenophobic policies like the Muslim ban imposed by the Trump administration, Amani has continued her work to change the conversation about race and religion in the United States by devoting herself fully to enterprises advocating for and supporting Muslim women. In 2016, *Muslim Girl* launched a care package subscription box, which included items like pepper spray, unfortunate essentials of survival for many Muslim women. And on March 27, 2017, *Muslim Girl* also launched a new day of celebration during Women's History Month: Muslim Women's Day.

Today, Amani continues to use her platform and visibility to give other Muslim women a chance to have their voices heard by each other and the larger culture. Through *Muslim Girl*, Amani continues to break new ground in media, entrepreneurship, representation, and discourse.

ALISSA LENTZ

ah-LEE-sah LENTZ

Born on July 14, 1989, in Novosibirsk, Siberia, Alissa Lentz and her family moved to the United States in 1992. As a Russian immigrant, she was bullied throughout childhood for not being an English speaker. At the time, Alissa was too young to understand that there was a language barrier between herself and the other kids, but she was old enough to feel there was something "different" about her. As a result, she became very shy and stopped speaking completely in elementary school. Alissa did not overcome this social anxiety until her friend drew a cartoon superhero on a sheet of paper and placed it inside her backpack with a note that said, "Speak Up!" Opening her backpack to see this simple yet powerful note of encouragement from a classmate became the inspiration for Alissa to find her voice.

Alissa's early experience with bullying caused her to have a fascination with human interaction and motivation. While studying business administration with an emphasis in entrepreneurship at Chapman University, Alissa became infatuated with the ways that marketing seized on psychology. To dive deeper into this interest, Alissa enrolled in an entrepreneurship course. In need of a business idea for a class project, Alissa thought back to her childhood for inspiration. She opened up about her experience with bullying and quickly learned that everyone in the class had experienced something that made them feel like an outsider. Alissa also realized that everyone in the class still carried the resulting trauma and insecurity with them. She decided she wanted to dedicate herself to providing encouragement to others struggling to speak up for themselves. Drawing inspiration from the memory of the encouraging note in her backpack, Alissa started HERO Backpacks because she didn't want anyone to feel the way that she felt growing up.

For Alissa, encouragement is the key to helping people overcome many of the obstacles they face, and HERO is designed to inspire confidence in everyone. Her backpack line is ethically sourced and manufactured, keeping to the company's mission of positivity. Each HERO backpack carries a card that shares an inspiring story of a hero, and 10 percent of the profits support organizations that take a stand for equality.

Alissa Lentz gives adults and young people the tools to feel empowered in an often unfriendly world. In 2018, she was named a *Forbes* "30 Under 30" for her work with HERO and children's advocacy. Today, Alissa speaks out against violence against women, bullying, and unethical manufacturing practices.

EMAN IDIL BARE

ee-MAN ih-DILL bar-REH

Eman Idil Bare was born on August 18, 1992, in Regina, Saskatchewan, and is of Somali and Ethiopian descent. Since she was fifteen, Eman has been passionate about fashion and storytelling and often dreamed of starting her own fashion line. While her goal seemed daunting, she held onto her aspiration, slowly created a business plan, and pursued journalism to hone her talent for storytelling.

While attending University of Regina School of Journalism, Eman was awarded the Canadian Television Investigative Journalism scholarship for outstanding student journalism. Following college, she gathered bylines by writing for *Teen Vogue*, *Huffington Post*, and **Muslim Girl**, and she became an on-air reporter for the Canadian Broadcasting Corporation.

Eman's career collided with her childhood dream when she became a fashion editor at *The Demureist*, a leading online outlet for fashion editorial dedicated to modest dressing. As a Muslim woman who chooses to dress modestly, this job allowed Eman to turn her dream into reality.

Like many entrepreneurs, Eman had to wear many hats in order to bring her dream into the real world. In launching her eponymous modest clothing brand, Eman Idil Designs, Eman served as the clothing line's designer, makeup artist, model, photographer, and social media manager. Eman Idil Designs launched in August 2016, and within days of its highly anticipated debut, products were swiftly selling out.

Eman is dedicated to creating designs for Muslim women and supporting environmental and economic sustainability in the fashion industry. All of the materials that go into Eman Idil Designs' garments are sourced from small, locally owned businesses in East Africa, North Africa, and South America. The clothing line provides fair and safe employment to refugee women from Somalia, Syria, Afghanistan, Haiti, and Nigeria who have resettled in the Canada and the United States. Each item purchased from Eman Idil Designs comes with a handwritten story of how that article of clothing or accessory came to be. At its core, Eman Idil Designs is a marriage of Eman's ability to tell stories through the form of self-expression that is fashion.

> "Muslim women shouldn't feel compelled to remove a part of their identity to appease others who don't understand their religion or culture."

IBTIHAJ MUHAMMAD

IB-tee-haj muh-HOMM-ud

Born December 4, 1985, in Maplewood, New Jersey, Ibtihaj Muhammad was an athlete from a young age, but as a young Muslim American who observed hijab, she often felt out of place in the world of sports. Her mother would add fabric to Ibtihaj's basketball uniforms to make them more modest, but the noticeable difference between her uniform and the uniforms of her peers prevented Ibtihaj from feeling like a part of the team.

When her mother realized that fencing uniforms, which were inherently modest, would allow her daughter to play a sport without feeling like she was out of place, she suggested Ibtihaj try out the sport. Ibtihaj began training at the Peter Westbrook Foundation, an organization dedicated to introducing fencing to underserved youth in New York City. Fencing allowed her to feel included, and Ibtihaj's passion for the sport grew as her unique talent became apparent. Ibtihaj's undeniable skill earned her a fencing scholarship to Duke University, where she completed dual degrees in international relations and African American studies.

At that point, Ibtihaj enjoyed the sport for its own sake and had become a skilled fencer. She was so talented that in 2010, she became a member of the National Fencing Team and embarked on her journey to the Olympics. In 2016, at the Rio Olympic Games, Ibtihaj shattered barriers by becoming the first American athlete to observe hijab during the international sporting event. She won a bronze medal, becoming the first Muslim American woman to win an Olympic medal and a role model for women and girls of faith around the world.

Ibtihaj's athletic abilities are matched by her bold entrepreneurial spirit and her commitment to providing options for Muslim girls that had not been available to her. Encouraged by her family members, Ibtihaj launched a clothing line, Louella, that provides a fresh spin on modest fashion. And in 2017, Ibtihaj became the model for Mattel's very first hijab-wearing Barbie, paving the way for a new era of culturally inclusive children's toys and providing Muslim girls with an important image of themselves.

Today Ibtihaj Muhammad is a speaker, athlete, and entrepreneur, encouraging young people everywhere never to give up and to stay true to themselves. Ibtihaj uses her unique voice and perspective to shed light on the experiences of black Muslims in the United States.

LESLIE MAC &
MARISSA JENAE JOHNSON

LEZ-lee MACK / mah-RISS-ah jeh-NAY JON-sun

Leslie Mac and Marissa Jenae Johnson are the cofounders of Safety Pin Box. When the duo launched the business in 2016, they powerfully disrupted the harmful idea that people who are oppressed must provide free labor in the form of education, physical work, and more to escape the hardship of oppression. By creating a business model around a monthly subscription box for white people striving to be allies in the fight for black lives, Leslie and Marissa took a revolutionary approach to community organizing that calls upon individuals in positions of **privilege** to use their wealth and access to compensate black women educators while also taking meaningful steps toward deconstructing white supremacy. For Leslie and Marissa, Safety Pin Box was the culmination of decades of organizing work rooted in a commitment to community.

Leslie Mac was raised in a large Jamaican family in Brooklyn, New York. Her childhood was influenced by the rich Caribbean culture of her family and community, and she spent her childhood summers in Jamaica with her grandparents learning about her heritage. One lesson Leslie's grandmother often repeated was, "We are here to help others, but not to be taken advantage of for the sake of service. Everyone is welcome in from the cold, but people have to earn their seat at your table." Even in her deep commitment to others, Leslie's grandmother prioritized her own well-being and safety. This lesson continues to guide Leslie and informed the approach of Safety Pin Box.

Leslie went on to a career as an activist dedicated to honoring black lives and working toward black liberation. She is a founding lead organizer of Black Lives of Unitarian Universalism and founder of the **Ferguson Response Network**, a tool for activists to connect worldwide and mobilize individuals to take part in on-the-ground actions and protests.

Marissa Jenae Johnson was born in Louisiana and grew up in a family that taught her the importance of a healthy work-life balance. One Saturday when Marissa was in high school, she woke up to make breakfast and prepare for a *Battlestar Galactica* marathon. Her father was getting ready for work as Marissa settled in for the day. As he put on his lanyard, he stopped to ask Marissa about her plans.

She told him about the TV marathon and joked about how he would miss out because of his work schedule. Marissa's dad called in sick to spend that Saturday hanging out with his daughter and watching the show. This instance taught her the importance of taking days off when you need them and that people should work to live, not live to work. These beliefs about enjoying life and prioritizing relationships above all else are a major reason that Marissa worked to build a business around her lifestyle, instead of trying to fit her life around her business.

In 2015, Marissa gained national attention as the cofounder of Black Lives Matter Seattle when she interrupted a presidential campaign speech delivered by Senator **Bernie Sanders**. The act drew both political and media attention to the ongoing crises faced by black people in the Seattle community and across the United States. In a subsequent interview on MSNBC, Marissa explained that organizers were demanding that Sanders take concrete action to protect the black community. Against a tidal wave of criticism for her use of the peaceful direct action tactic of interrupting a major political speech, Marissa continued her activism and became a well-known activist in the **Movement for Black Lives**.

Leslie and Marissa met as organizers in the fight for black liberation and founded Safety Pin Box in the wake of the 2016 presidential election, when many white allies took to wearing safety pins to profess their dedication to the liberation of people of color. This act showed that many people, though not a part of **marginalized groups**, were willing to step up. Unfortunately, the act of wearing a safety pin had little impact on actually improving the conditions of oppressed folks and demonstrated how people from privileged groups often misunderstand how they can actually make a difference. Each month's box contained allyship tasks as well as educational materials that invited individuals in positions of privilege to educate themselves about the role they play in maintaining white supremacy and injustice. Each month the company also provided a one-time financial gift to black women activists and organizers committed to community liberation work through a program called Black Women Being.

Marissa, Leslie, and Safety Pin Box have been celebrated for representing a new form of support and advocacy, and have been featured in media such as *Essence*, NPR, and BBC News. Though Safety Pin Box was retired in 2018, the two continue to work as speakers, activists, and **grassroots** organizers.

RIHANNA

ree-AH-nah

Born Robyn Rihanna Fenty on February 20, 1988, Rihanna grew up on the Caribbean island of Barbados. As a teenager, struggling through her parent's recent divorce, Rihanna found strength in her musical talents. At the age of fifteen, she scored an audition with a notable music producer and began recording a demo album.

In 2004, Rihanna recorded the party anthem "Pon de Replay," and her life changed forever. The song caught the attention of a myriad of record labels, including Def Jam Records and the label's then-president Jay-Z. Rihanna signed with Def Jam at sixteen and embarked on her journey in the music industry. "Pon de Replay" peaked at the number two spot on the Billboard Hot 100, instantly launching Rihanna's career. By 2012, Rihanna had released seven albums and won six Grammy Awards.

In the midst of her meteoric success, Rihanna began using her fame to advance social justice. In 2006 she founded the Believe Foundation, which helps terminally ill children, and the Clara Lionel Foundation, founded in 2012, is Rihanna's most recent endeavor in giving back. Named in honor of her grandparents, Clara and Lionel Braithwaite, it supports and funds groundbreaking education, health, and emergency response programs around the world for young people. Rihanna stated, "The notion that millions of kids are desperate to go to school and are not given the opportunity, is something I cannot accept." During the foundation's first year, it established the Clara Braithwaite Center for Oncology and Nuclear Medicine at Queen Elizabeth Hospital in Barbados to address the limited access to quality cancer screening and treatment equipment. In 2016, the foundation launched the Clara Lionel Foundation Global Scholarship Program to provide financial assistance to young people from the Caribbean and South America who come the United States to pursue higher education.

In 2017, Rihanna rocked the beauty industry to its core when she launched the inclusive, cruelty-free cosmetic line Fenty Beauty. Among a number of high quality and affordable products, Fenty Beauty offered a previously unheard-of forty shades of foundation at its launch. The diverse Fenty foundations include shades that work for people with albinism to those with deep ebony skin tones. Following the makeup line launch, other cosmetic companies scrambled to match the level of inclusivity Rihanna had attained.

Today, Rihanna is an international multi-platinum recording artist, entrepreneur, philanthropist, and advocate for youth.

SHANNON COULTER

SHA-nun COLE-ter

Shannon Coulter was born on October 21, 1971, in Fort Wayne, Indiana, and grew up in San Francisco, California. When she was seven, Shannon began to demonstrate a knack for leadership and community organizing when she created an all-girls club called the Ladybugs. The mission of the club was to pick up trash from the forest floor, though given the young age of the members, equal time was spent executing the club's mission and playing tag. But it was a formative experience and her first work as an activist and as a steward of nature.

As an adult, Shannon attended Penn State University and went on to a career leading marketing efforts at a solar energy startup. With a love for nature that began in her youth, solar energy was appealing to Shannon and the experience of working at a startup taught her about the influences and motivations people need to take action. She leveraged this knowledge to become a successful organizer and advocate. Shannon learned that individuals need specific steps to take action and to feel connected to a larger movement.

"Things may be close at the polling place, but they're not close at the cash register."

While her initial profession had elements of advocacy, the rise of presidential candidate Donald Trump inspired Shannon to leave her marketing career for one of full-time activism. On October 11, 2016, in the wake of the release of vulgar statements made by Trump, Shannon put her marketing skills to work by launching the #GrabYourWallet movement to boycott retailers selling products from the various companies owned by Trump and his family. The hashtag exploded on social media, boasting impressions in the billions. Utilizing free and accessible online resources like Google Docs and social media, the Grab Your Wallet website used spreadsheets and an open interface to communicate the progress of the boycott effort and help others get involved.

While many of the progressive organizations known collectively as The Resistance began following suit in protesting Trump products immediately after the 2016 US elections, Shannon's efforts began before it. Thanks to her efforts, the #GrabYourWallet boycott has grown into a movement and central resource for using collective consumer power to push for a more ethical and responsible market.

TEGAN & SARA

TEE-gun and SARE-ah

Born on September 19, 1980, in Calgary, Alberta, Sara Quin and Tegan Quin are identical twin sisters and bandmates in the rock and indie-pop duo, Tegan and Sara. While today they are dedicated advocates of queer youth, realizing their respective queer identities was a journey of self-discovery. For Sara, the summer before seventh grade was when she discovered her queer identity. Like many LGBTQ youth, at first Sara was intimidated by her attraction to other girls, concerned she was doing something wrong and would not be accepted. Thankfully, Sara found affirmation in the music of Ani DiFranco and Melissa Etheridge. Similarly, Tegan, found a role model in the androgynous Canadian musician, k.d. lang, and came out during her senior year of high school. In 1995, at the age of fifteen, they began exploring their musical talents. Three years later, the two formed their signature band, Tegan and Sara.

From the beginning, part of their mission as openly lesbian artists was to provide the kind of support and role modeling that had been so important to them as young women, and to use their music to openly affirm queer experiences. For many members of the LGBTQ community and especially young people, Tegan and Sara's songs provide acknowledgment and representation of LGBTQ experiences and lives.

Their 2012 double platinum single, "Closer," became a coming out anthem for LGBTQ youth the world over, and Sara and Tegan have become the role models and mentors they sought out in their adolescence.

In October 2016, the duo launched the Tegan and Sara Foundation, which utilizes their star power to help LGBTQ organizations in the United States and Canada build capacity through grants and volunteers. To address the devastation following the 2016 mass shooting that took the lives of forty-nine people at Pulse Nightclub in Orlando, Florida, funds from the foundation went toward expanding counseling services for queer youth in Orlando. The foundation has also supported the Audre Lorde Project's community support initiatives and resources for queer people of color in New York City.

For the tenth anniversary of the release of their 2007 album *The Con*, Tegan and Sara collaborated with seventeen artists to recreate the hit album in *The Con X: Covers*. Going on tour to celebrate the album's anniversary, they donated a portion of the proceeds from album and concert sales to their foundation. As Sara and Tegan accumulate success as international stars, they remain steadfast to their commitment to social justice.

CHAPTER
8

THE REVOLUTION
IS NOW

One of the most challenging aspects of growing up is discovering the many injustices of the world. Children are just beginning to learn about themselves and are completely innocent to the biases held by society for centuries. But before kids even learn basic math, they absorb cultural norms that reinforce the toxic boundaries society has created to keep others down. In childhood, we learn that blue is "for boys" and that pink is "for girls." We learn that girls should be quiet and passive, while boys are allowed to be boisterous and forceful. We learn to put people in boxes, we learn to discriminate, and later we are tasked with unlearning these toxic lessons. There has been a moment in each of our lives when we first experienced discrimination. For children who are told that their future is boundless, witnessing injustice for the first time can be devastating to both confidence and morale.

Fortunately, because of the work of the people in this book and others like them, these boundaries are gradually being broken down, and young people today are forging a reality that meaningfully includes everyone. Today's young people are growing up in an era where it is becoming more normal to push back against boundaries and to recognize and fight against injustice.

Every day, young people around the world are boldly rejecting the stigma society places upon them and others. Young change-makers demonstrate that becoming aware of social inequalities is the first step to a lifetime of activism and advocacy.

Changing the world often starts out with small acts of revolution. Eight-year-old **Mari Copeny** didn't know what it meant to be an activist when she stood up for her entire community and penned a heartfelt letter to President **Barack Obama**. **Jazz Jennings** was only six years old when she became a prominent voice for **transgender** youth everywhere. When she was ten, **Marley Dias** decided to take her frustrations about the lack of diversity in children's books and transform that energy into a national dialogue about representation. Declaring who you are in a world that would rather fit you into a box or under a label is a profound act of revolution, especially for a very young person.

Any of us can start making a change in our communities today. In "The Revolution is Now," we will learn about youth activists born in or after the year 2000 who are already making a profound difference in their communities and the world, and who show that you can be an activist no matter your age or experience.

JAZZ JENNINGS

Jazz Jennings was born on October 6, 2000. Since childhood, she has been a revolutionary force for change against conventions of gender expression and identity. At age six, Jazz and her family began to boldly speak out about her transgender identity. In 2007, she appeared on national television with Barbara Walters and became one of the youngest transgender children to appear in media. Later that year, Jazz and her parents, Jeanette and Greg, founded the TransKids Purple Rainbow Foundation to provide resources to transgender youth and their families.

Jazz is no stranger to discrimination. For five years, she wasn't allowed to use the girls' restroom in her elementary school. For transgender people, everything from gender dysphoria to threats of violence can result when outdated notions of gender overrule the basic human right to use the bathroom that aligns with one's gender identity. From eight to eleven, Jazz was also banned from competing with her school's girls' soccer team by her state. After a long battle, the United States Soccer Federation (USSF) ordered her home state to lift the ban. As a result of the discrimination that Jazz was forced to endure, the USSF created a policy to include all transgender athletes who want to play soccer in the United States.

In 2011, a documentary about her life and family, *I Am Jazz: A Family in Transition*, premiered on the Oprah Winfrey Network (OWN), helping raise public awareness of the issues faced by transgender kids and their families. In 2015, the Jennings family partnered with TLC to produce the GLAAD award-winning television series of the same name, which provided a more intimate window into the realities of growing up as a transgender teen in a society committed to reinforcing archaic expectations around gender.

In making an indelible mark on the fight for LGBTQ equality, Jazz has been widely recognized for her contributions. She was named as one of *Time* magazine's "25 Most Influential Teens" in 2014 and 2015, and is the youngest person to ever be featured in *Out* magazine's "Out 100" and *Advocate*'s "40 under 40." As an author, Jazz cowrote a children's picture book titled *I Am Jazz*, and in 2016, published her memoir, *Being Jazz: My Life as a (Transgender) Teen*.

Jazz Jennings's activism and visibility continue to disrupt society's expectations of gender expression. Today, Jazz speaks at universities, medical schools, conferences, conventions, and symposiums all over the United States about her lived experiences as a transgender youth, as she has since she was six years old.

MARI COPENY

MARR-ee CO-peh-nee

Born on July 6, 2007, in Flint, Michigan, Mari Copeny is an activist whose everyday mission is to remind people that access to clean water is a basic human right.

In April 2014, elected officials in Flint reassured its citizens that their water was safe to drink despite complaints from residents about the odor, color, and taste of the water running from their taps. Lab tests began to reveal unacceptably high levels of lead in Flint's tap water and in blood tests of young children, yet elected officials in the city took few actions to curb the growing public health crisis. In December 2015, well over a year after the residents of Flint began to express concern and outrage, the city finally declared an emergency. Corroding pipes had contaminated the water supply with lethal amounts of lead and other heavy metals. The entire Flint community became preoccupied by the health consequences they would undoubtedly face, yet media coverage of the disaster was sparse.

Eight years old at the time, Flint resident Mari Copeny wrote a letter to President Barack Obama, challenging him to come to her hometown and bear witness to the crisis she and her community faced. Her letter quickly gained national attention after it was published in the *Los Angeles Times*. Mari forced the American public to reckon with the reality faced by a vast yet silenced segment of the country. President Obama responded to Mari and visited Flint on May 4, 2016. Obama's visit and the visibility of an eight-year-old girl taking matters of political failure into her own hands resulted in a wave of increased donations and resources to Flint as local lawmakers faced increased scrutiny.

Mari became a full-fledged activist before she even knew what being an activist meant. She did not hesitate to reach out to President Obama though her family worried that she might not receive a response. She was just a kid experiencing a seemingly insurmountable hardship and wanted the president to do something about it. Empowered by the fact that one small act resulted in increased awareness and resources for her community, Mari continues to grow her personal platform and use social media as a tool to raise awareness. With the support of her family and a legion of mentors around the United States, Mari also works to provide backpacks and school supplies to underserved children and speaks out against bullying and violence. Her mission emerges from her desire to be a carefree kid, liberated from the fears of water contamination.

MARLEY DIAS

MAR-lee DYE-us

Named after Jamaican reggae artist Bob Marley, Marley Dias was born on January 3, 2005, in Philadelphia, Pennsylvania. She grew up in New Jersey and quickly grew into an intellectually curious young person and avid reader. Unfortunately, as Marley sought new books to read, she struggled to find books with characters she could identify with and who looked like her—a young black girl. Many of the books she was assigned to read in school were stories about white boys and dogs. Marley talked to her mother about this lack of diversity as it evolved from a concern to a frustration. After an inspiring conversation with her mother, Marley decided to launch a book drive to resolve a problem that she and so many girls across the world were facing.

When she was ten years old, Marley launched #1000BlackGirlBooks in the fall of 2015 with the mission of collecting and donating over a thousand books that featured black girls as protagonists to local libraries and community centers across the country. When Marley first started thinking about how to address the lack of books featuring young black female characters, she consciously chose to address the problem like an agent of social change, choosing a method that benefited people beyond herself, and brought the issue to light in the public eye. By 2017, she had surpassed her goal of a thousand books many times over, receiving donations and having content created specifically in response to her program.

In 2017, Marley spoke on the same stage as business leaders and activists at the Forbes Women's Summit in New York City about the movement for youth literacy and increased representation that she had created just a few years prior. In 2018, Marley became a published author to show young people how to get involved in positive social change. In her book, *Marley Dias Gets It Done: And So Can You!*, Marley details how she identified a problem facing her and sought to make a solution that benefitted the whole community. Marley isn't content with being an activist by herself; she wants to show other kids that everyone can create positive social change and make their dreams and aspirations come true.

> "I'm working to create a space where it feels easy to include and imagine black girls and make black girls like me the main characters of our lives."

TAYLOR RICHARDSON

TAY-lur RICH-ard-sin

Born on July 15, 2003, Taylor Denise Richardson—also known as Astronaut StarBright—came to the national stage due to her philanthropic efforts to ensure that girls across the United States could see the 2016 movie *Hidden Figures* free of charge. The film tells the inspiring story of pioneering NASA scientists and mathematicians Dorothy Vaughan, Mary Jackson, and Katherine Johnson. From a young age, Taylor had aspirations of one day being a scientist, engineer, and an astronaut. Despite having interest and the opportunity to visit NASA space centers, Taylor feared that she could not be an astronaut because of her race and gender. Beyond her idol Dr. Mae Jemison, the first African American woman to go into space, Taylor rarely saw other women of color in the fields that interested her.

In May 2016, at age 12, Taylor had the honor of meeting Dr. Jemison when she introduced her to the graduates of the HBCU Clark Atlanta University as their commencement speaker. Later that year, Taylor was invited to the first-ever White House United State of Women Summit hosted by the Obama administration to learn more about gender equality for girls and women.

> "Girls need to know if we do the work and stick together like these women did, we can accomplish many things. One day maybe one of us will even be a president!"

In December 2016, Taylor was invited back to the White House to attend a special private screening and discussion of *Hidden Figures* where the cast, producer, book author, and First Lady Michelle Obama spoke. This motivated her to raise funds to allow hundreds of girls to see the movie and receive a copy of the book the film was based on. In 2017, Taylor raised over $20,000 to sponsor free screenings of the film for over a thousand kids in Florida, Virginia, Maryland, Georgia, and South Carolina. The campaign was such a huge success it inspired national campaigns for screenings in seventy-two cities, with twenty-eight of the campaigns raising over $120,000. In 2018, Taylor doubled down on her effort to help her peers see themselves on the big screen by partnering with Walt Disney Studios and GoFundMe to bring as many young people as possible to see Ava DuVernay's *A Wrinkle in Time*. Oprah Winfrey matched the donations made to Taylor's campaign for a total of $100,000 for young people to see the film.

Today, Taylor Richardson inspires children and adults alike with her activism, public speaking, and selfless philanthropy.

YARA SHAHIDI

YAH-rah sha-HEE-dee

Actor and activist Yara Shahidi was born on February 20, 2000. Yara spent her early years in Minneapolis, Minnesota before her family moved to Southern California for her father's work in photography and her mother's career as an actor. Yara's family heritage is a blend of African American, Iranian, and Native American Choctaw ancestry.

Following her parents' footsteps in the entertainment industry, Yara started her career as a model during childhood, often joining her mother on the set of commercials. In 2009, Yara landed a role on the ABC comedy show *In the Motherhood*, and that same year made her film debut opposite comedian and actor Eddie Murphy in Paramount Pictures' *Imagine That.*

In 2014, Yara joined the cast of ABC's Emmy-nominated comedy series *black-ish*, which tackles difficult subjects like racial discrimination, **privilege**, class, and **police violence**. While starring in the show, Yara made a conscious choice to use her growing platform to fight for human rights and to advocate for justice. Her work on the show earned her an **NAACP** Image Award for Best Supporting Actress in a Comedy in 2017. Following her role on *black-ish*, Freeform greenlit a spin-off series called *grown-ish* which continues her character's storyline with lessons about the complexities of young adulthood and social injustice through the lens of humor and levity.

In August 2017, Yara gave a powerful speech at TEDxTeen on the harms of negative media representation and the ways in which positive portrayals of black people through shows like *black-ish* and the spin-off show *grown-ish* are combatting those stereotypes. Yara expressed her goal of breaking down the stereotypes of black people that mainstream media provides.

Yara uses her star power to shine a light on the crises facing her generation like voter suppression, gun violence, and **xenophobia**. The emerging activist and award-winning actor has already interviewed cultural icons like Congressman **John Lewis**, **Hillary Clinton**, and **Oprah Winfrey**. In these dialogues Yara often focuses on the importance of the power of young people and the need for everyone to be involved in the movement for change.

> **"What's so cool about my generation is that being socially aware is ingrained in who we are."**

CONCLUSION

———

Before I got to college and began taking African American studies and women's and gender studies courses, I had never heard of **Sylvia Rivera**, **Marsha P. Johnson**, or **Audre Lorde**. Learning about people like these changed the vision I had of recent history and made it a more vivid tapestry that moved beyond the mythologized accomplishments of white men. Growing up, I didn't see people like myself or my family represented in history books. Why were black people only shown in the context of slavery? Where were the women of color? The **LGBTQ** folks? The lack of diversity was noticeable. My history lessons from elementary through high school painted a troubling picture that left me without role models with whom I could identify. In my experience of the world, I saw people from every walk of life making positive change in their communities. Why were their contributions to history not celebrated? Why were their stories left untold?

I hope that *Modern HERstory* is a meaningful step in the right direction, helping address the issue of historical erasure by centering those who are most often left out of our collective history. I wanted more than anything to reveal the important work, dedication, and contributions of our recent foremothers and highlight the progress being made by icons in the world today. By reflecting the complex and nuanced reality of our world, I hope that this book can provide a mirror in which young people can see themselves and understand that they too can make history.

GLOSSARY

TERMS, EVENTS, AND PHRASES

Here is some basic information about notable terms, events, and phrases used throughout this book.

1963 MARCH ON WASHINGTON: Also known as the March on Washington for Jobs and Freedom, this protest was organized by A. Philip Randolph and Bayard Rustin. The march consisted of a coalition of civil rights organizations under the mission of "jobs and freedom." The August 28 event drew more than 200,000 participants and is remembered for the speech "I Have a Dream," delivered by Dr. Martin Luther King, Jr. in front of the Lincoln Memorial.

1983 MARCH FOR EQUALITY AND AGAINST RACISM: Known in French as *Marche pour l'égalité et contre le racism*, these demonstrations were organized by clergy in France following a series of racist hate crimes against African and Arab people during the summer of 1983 in Lyon. Drawing upon the legacy of Dr. Martin Luther King, Jr. in the United States, the demonstrations are considered to be the first national anti-racist movement in France and lasted from October 15 to December 3, 1983.

ANTI-LGBTQ: The discrimination against, prejudiced treatment of, and stereotyping of LGBTQ people (also known as homophobia and/or transphobia).

ANTI-MUSLIM: The discrimination against, prejudiced treatment of, and stereotyping of Muslim people (also known as Islamophobia).

BISEXUAL: A person who has the capacity to form enduring physical, romantic, and/or emotional attractions to those of the same gender or to those of another gender. People may experience this attraction in differing ways and degrees over their lifetime.

BLACK PANTHER PARTY: Originally called the Black Panther Party for Self-Defense, the Black Panther Party was a revolutionary political party, founded in 1966 in Oakland, California, by Huey Newton and Bobby Seale. The Black Panther Party instituted free health clinics, free meals for communities, and free breakfast and lunch for children at public schools.

BLACK TWITTER: Defined by Feminista Jones as a collective of active, primarily African American Twitter users who have created a virtual community that participates in continuous real-time conversations.

BLACKFACE: A racist form of theatrical makeup (including literal black paint) used by a non-black or light skinned person to "represent" caricatures of black people.

CAME OUT: *See* coming out.

CEREBRAL PALSY: A neurological disorder caused by complications or brain injury during infant or child brain development.

CISGENDER: An adjective used to describe a person who identifies with the gender they were assigned with at birth.

CIVIL RIGHTS MOVEMENT: The movement of leaders, groups, and direct-action strategies used from 1954 to 1968 with the goal of ending racial segregation, race- and class-based discrimination, and protecting the civil and human rights of marginalized Americans in the United States. The Civil Rights Movement was notable for the use of non-violence and the commitment to addressing the injustices of poverty and war.

CLOSETED: A state of not being out about one's LGBTQ identity. Closeted refers to the phrase of "being in the closet" and can also be described simply as "not out" about one's LGBTQ identity. Many people cannot be out due to safety, fear of rejection, violence, or harassment.

COLORISM: Defined by author Alice Walker as prejudice in favor of lighter skin color within and between groups and cultures.

COMING OUT: A lifelong process of finding self-definition. People forge an LGBTQ identity first to themselves and then they may reveal it to others. Publicly sharing one's identity may or may not be part of coming out.

CRITICAL RACE THEORY: A way of understanding educational research and discourse by placing race at the center of the conversation. It was officially defined by Kimberlé Crenshaw in the *Harvard Law Review* article, "Race, Reform, and Retrenchment: Transformation and Legitimation in Anti-Discrimination Law."

CULTURAL APPROPRIATION: The act of borrowing or commodifying elements from a culture that is not your own, especially without showing that you understand or respect this culture.

EPILEPSY: A neurological disorder that causes disturbances in nerve activity in the brain and causes seizures.

EXECUTIVE ORDER: In the United States, the presidential power to issue rules to the military or other part of the executive branch of the government which must be obeyed as law.

FEMINIST: A person who believes or participates in feminist movements that seek to implement the equality of genders, especially in the economic, social, and political realms.

GAY: A gender-neutral adjective used to describe people whose enduring physical, romantic, and/or emotional attractions are to people of the same gender.

GENDER: A broad term used to define elements of the human experience. There are many gender identities and expressions beyond the binary notions of man and woman or masculinity and femininity. Gender is not defined by a person's biology or body. The idea that gender is limited to a binary emerged from European colonization. In many pre-colonial African societies, for example, gender was not a constructed form of social categorization. Washington is the first state in the United States to allow for the birth identification of Gender X, which encompasses a gender that is not exclusively male or female. To learn more about gender see *The Invention of*

Women: Making an African Sense of Western Gender Discourses by Oyèrónkẹ́ Oyěwùmí and *Gender Trouble: Feminism and the Subversion of Identity* by Judith Butler.

GENDER EXPRESSION: The ways in which a person expresses their gender identity, often through dress, appearance, or pronoun usage.

GENDER IDENTITY: A person's internal, deeply held sense of their gender.

GENDER-NONCONFORMING: A term used to describe some people whose gender expression is different from conventional expectations of masculinity and femininity. Not all gender-nonconforming people identify as transgender, nor are all transgender people gender-nonconforming.

GENDERQUEER: A term used by some people who experience their gender identity and/or gender expression as falling outside the categories of male and female.

GRASSROOTS: A type of movement that mobilizes everyday people as the leaders of a social, political, or economic movement.

HARASSMENT: Unwanted repetitive behavior that is offensive in nature. Harassment can take place online, on the street (also known as street harassment or cat-calling), in places of worship or learning, in workplaces, and in the home.

HARD OF HEARING: Refers to someone who has difficulty hearing. Someone can be hard of hearing since birth or due to hearing loss later in life.

HARLEM RENAISSANCE: The period from 1910 to 1930 that saw the proliferation of black and African American creative works including paintings, poetry, essays, books, performances, music, and more.

HBCU (HISTORICALLY BLACK COLLEGES AND UNIVERSITIES): Colleges, universities, and other institutions of higher education in the United States that were established before the Civil Rights Act of 1964 to address the lack of educational institutions that served the black community due to anti-black racism and segregation.

HETERONORMATIVE: The ideology that promotes heterosexuality as the normal or preferred sexual orientation above all other sexual orientations.

HIJAB: A head covering worn in public by some Muslim people.

HIV/AIDS: HIV is an acronym for human immunodeficiency virus. HIV is a virus that attacks the immune system, which is our body's natural defense against illness. AIDS is an acronym for acquired immunodeficiency syndrome. AIDS is not a virus but a set of symptoms caused by HIV.

HUMAN TRAFFICKING: The sale and trade of human beings for the purposes of forced sexual and/or economic exploitation.

INTEGRATE: The process of bringing different groups of people together as equals in society.

INTERSECTIONALITY: A way of understanding the various forms of oppression in society and the ways they impact us according to overlapping identities. The term was coined by black legal scholar and feminist Kimberlé Crenshaw in her 1989 essay "Demarginalizing the Intersection of Race and Sex: A Black Feminist Critique of Antidiscrimination Doctrine, Feminist Theory and Antiracist Politics."

JIM CROW: Refers to the policies and laws that enforced racial segregation throughout the southern United States following end of chattel slavery. Jim Crow laws segregated schools, drinking fountains, bathrooms, and other facilities with infamous "Whites Only" and "Colored Only" signs, rampant police violence, and domestic terrorism.

LATINX: A gender–neutral umbrella term that describes people of many countries, cultures, and races who are united by a shared history as descendants of the colonization of Central and South America. "Latinx" is often used in lieu of the gendered "Latino" or "Latina."

LESBIAN: A woman whose enduring physical, romantic, and/or emotional attraction is to other women.

LESBIAN, GAY, BISEXUAL, TRANSGENDER AND QUEER (LGBTQ) RIGHTS MOVEMENT: A social movement for the equal acceptance of LGBTQ people in society. Following the Stonewall Riots in 1969, the LGBTQ Rights Movement began using direct action mobilization to confront homophobic and transphobic legislation and policies.

LGBTQ: An acronym of lesbian, gay, bisexual, transgender, and queer. The acronym is often expanded to LGBTQIA+ which includes intersex, asexual, and other groups that fall along the spectrum of gender and sexual orientation.

LITTLE ROCK NINE: Following the decision in the 1954 Supreme Court case of Brown v. Board of Education, racial segregation in schools was deemed unconstitutional. Nine students from Little Rock, Arkansas, volunteered with a local chapter of the NAACP to be the first students to integrate Little Rock Central High School. The nine students included Ernest Green, Elizabeth Eckford, Jefferson Thomas, Terrence Roberts, Carlotta Walls LaNier, Minnijean Brown, Gloria Ray Karlmark, Thelma Mothershed, and Melba Pattillo Beals. After failed attempts to enter the school against the mobs of people committed to racial segregation, President Dwight D. Eisenhower sent US Army troops to accompany the students to school for protection. Nonetheless, the nine students were subjected to a year of physical and verbal abuse and harassment by their white peers.

MARGINALIZED GROUPS: Refers to groups of people and communities that have been historically denied rights and representation in society.

MICROAGGRESSION: A term coined by Derald Sue to refer to "brief and commonplace daily verbal, behavioral, or environmental indignities, whether intentional or unintentional, that communicate hostile, derogatory, or negative racial slights and insults toward people of color."

MILLION WOMAN MARCH: A march to bring empowerment and unity to women of the African diaspora across nationality, religion, or economic status. It was held on October 25, 1997 in Philadelphia, Pennsylvania, and organized by black women activists led by Phile Chionesu. Speakers included South African human rights activist Winnie Madikizela-Mandela; daughters of Malcolm X, Attallah and Ilyasah Shabazz; representative Maxine Waters and actor Jada Pinkett Smith.

MUSLIM BAN: The colloquial term for Executive Order 13769 issued by President Donald Trump on January 27, 2017. The executive order banned entry to the United States by people from seven majority-Muslim countries—Iran, Iraq, Libya, Somalia, Sudan, Syria, and Yemen—for ninety days. In response, Americans took to the street in protest at airports and courthouses to show outrage at the forty-fifth president's discriminatory action. On February 3, 2017, a nationwide temporary restraining order was issued in the case of Washington v. Trump, which was upheld by the United States Court of Appeals for the Ninth Circuit on February 9, 2017. Thanks to the political pressure and swift legal action by US Courts, the Department of Homeland Security was prevented from enforcing the order and the State Department reinstated visas that had been previously revoked.

NONBINARY: An adjective to describe the gender identity of people who fall somewhere in between the masculine and feminine ends of the gender identity spectrum, or are completely outside of the gender binary, or identify as neither man nor woman.

OSTEOGENESIS IMPERFECTA: A genetic disorder characterized by bones that break easily, often from little or no apparent cause.

PATRIARCHY: A social structure that prioritizes men in positions of leadership, moral authority, and economic control.

POLICE VIOLENCE: One of many forms of police misconduct involving undue violence by police members on members of the public.

PRIVILEGE: The benefits or advantages that certain groups of people are given or denied in social power structures. In 1988, Peggy McIntosh published the article "White Privilege and Male Privilege: A Personal Account of Coming to See Correspondences through Work on Women's Studies," which informs current understanding of social privilege.

QUEER: An adjective used by some people whose sexual orientation is not exclusively heterosexual and/or whose gender identity is not cisgender.

RACISM: The discrimination against, prejudiced treatment of, or stereotyping of people of color on the basis of race.

RAPE CULTURE: A social ideology that normalizes sexual violence through victim blaming, sexual objectification, and denial about the reality of sexual abuse and rape.

REFUGEE: An individual who has been displaced by war, conflict, natural disaster, terrorism, or other event that prevents them from returning home safely.

THE RESISTANCE: A movement of progressive, predominantly white organizations that began immediately following the 2016 United States presidential election.

SAY HER NAME: An initiative started in 2015 by Kimberlé Crenshaw to focus on documenting and uplifting the stories of black women, like Sandra Bland, who had been killed by police. It includes a research brief on the types of violence women of color and black women face from police and other institutions, and recommendations for ways to engage communities in conversations about black women's experiences of police violence.

SEGREGATION: Refers to the separation or isolation of groups based on race, gender, or class.

SEX WORKER: An employee of the direct sexual services industry.

SEX-POSITIVE: Describes progressive and tolerant attitudes toward sex and sexuality.

SEXISM: The discrimination against, prejudiced treatment of, or stereotyping of women.

SEXUAL ABUSE: Sexual abuse, or molestation, is unwanted sexual behavior by one person towards another.

SEXUAL ASSAULT: Sexual assault, or rape, is when a person is coerced or physically forced to participate in a sexual act against their will. Sexual assault can also refer to the nonconsensual sexual touching of a person.

STREET TRANSVESTITE ACTION REVOLUTIONARIES (STAR): An LGBTQ street activist organization founded in 1970 by Sylvia Rivera and Marsha P. Johnson to address the rates of homelessness experienced by LGBTQ youth in New York City. It is not currently active.

STUDENT NONVIOLENT COORDINATING COMMITTEE: The Student Nonviolent Coordinating Committee (SNCC) transformed the framework of the Civil Rights Movement. With SNCC, young activists and organizers used grassroots organizing techniques to activate communities to seize power in the face of oppression. It is not currently active.

TRANSGENDER: An umbrella term for people whose gender identity differs from the gender they were assigned at birth. Can be abbreviated as "trans." When referring to a person who is transgender, always use the descriptive term preferred by that person (which may or may not be "transgender").

TERF (TRANS-EXCLUSIONARY RADICAL FEMINIST): A term used to differentiate true radical feminists (who rightfully include trans people in their feminism) from transphobic and biased "radical" feminists who exclude and denigrate trans people.

TITLE IX: An amendment to the Higher Education Act in 1972, which disallowed discrimination on the basis of gender by universities and colleges that receive federal funding. The amendment made changes to both the athletic and academic arenas: before Title IX, women's and men's sports were not equally funded and there was no formal prohibition of gender-based discrimination.

VITILIGO: A condition which causes depigmentation of the skin.

WAR ON DRUGS: A policing program started by President Nixon in the 1970s and bolstered by President Ronald Reagan in 1982. The War on Drugs resulted in the criminalization of marginalized communities and drove mass incarceration, which resulted in a vast increase in the number of incarcerated individuals from 1980 through today.

WHITEWASHING: The act of casting a white actor as a person or character who is historically or canonically a person of color.

XENOPHOBIA: The discrimination against, prejudiced treatment of, and stereotyping of people perceived to be foreign.

GLOSSARY

PEOPLE

Here is more information about some of the notable people mentioned throughout this book.

AALIYAH (1979–2001): A black American singer, model, and actor from Brooklyn, New York. Her career lasted from 1991 until her untimely death in 2001 at age 22.

AL SHARPTON (1954–): A black American civil rights activist, commentator, minister, and former White House advisor from New York City.

ALICE WALKER (1944–): A black American feminist, novelist, and activist known for writing the award-winning novel, *The Color Purple* (1982).

ALICE WONG (1974–): An Asian American disability rights activist who founded the Disability Visibility Project, an initiative dedicated to recording, amplifying, and sharing disability stories and culture created in 2014.

ALTON STERLING (1979–2016): A black American father who, at thirty-seven, was shot several times at close range while held down on the ground by two Baton Rouge Police Department officers in Baton Rouge, Louisiana. The viral video of his death sparked protests of police violence across the country under the call to action #blacklivesmatter.

DR. ANGELA DAVIS (1944–): A black American lesbian political activist, educator, and author from Birmingham, Alabama, known for her activism beginning the 1960s and continuing to the present day. She is the author of *Women, Race & Class* (1981), *The Meaning of Freedom: And Other Difficult Dialogues* (2012), *Freedom Is a Constant Struggle* (2015), and many other books.

ANI DIFRANCO (1970–): A feminist American singer, poet, and musician known for her alternative rock music and advocacy for women's and LGBTQ rights.

ANITA HILL (1956–): A black American attorney and legal scholar. She is the author of *Reimagining Equality: Stories of Gender, Race, and Finding Home* (2011) and *Speaking Truth to Power* (1998).

ASHA BANDELE: The prolific and award-winning author of *Daughter* (2003) and *The Prisoner's Wife* (2000), and coauthor of Patrisse Cullors's memoir, *When They Call You a Terrorist: A Black Lives Matter Memoir* (2018).

AUDRE LORDE (1934–1992): A black American writer, womanist, and civil rights activist from Harlem, New York. She is the author of *Zami: A New Spelling of My Name* (1982), *Sister Outsider* (1984), and *I Am Your Sister* (1985).

BARACK HUSSEIN OBAMA (1961–): A black American politician who was elected as the forty-fourth president of the United States, serving from 2009 to 2017. Obama is the first African American president in United States history. Following his presidency, he established the Obama Foundation to inspire and empower young leaders and civic innovators to change their world. He is married to Michelle Robinson Obama.

BARBARA WALTERS (1929 –): A white American producer, journalist, and news anchor known for being the first woman to co-anchor a network evening news program. Using her signature interview style, she has provided an intimate view into the lives of heads of state and cultural icons including Fidel Castro, Anna Wintour, Margaret Thatcher, and more. She has hosted *Today*, *The View*, *20/20*, and *ABC World News Tonight*.

BELL HOOKS (1952–): A black American author, feminist, and social activist. She is the author of *Feminist Theory: From Margin to Center* (1984), *Talking Back: Thinking Feminist, Thinking Black* (1988), and *Feminism Is for Everybody* (2000).

DR. BERNICE KING (1963–): A black American activist and faith leader and the daughter of Dr. Martin Luther King, Jr., and Coretta Scott King. She is the chief executive officer of The King Center and a mentor to youth activists globally.

BERNIE SANDERS (1941–): A white American independent politician and United States senator from Vermont.

BEYONCÉ KNOWLES-CARTER (1981–): A black American cultural icon, singer, dancer, actor, and entrepreneur. She is the sister of Solange Knowles. Born in Houston, Texas, Beyoncé rose to prominence as the lead singer of Destiny's Child before embarking on her award-winning solo career in 2003.

Beyoncé is an advocate for women and girls, and a philanthropist who has contributed to a variety of causes for social good.

BILL CLINTON (1946–): A white American politician who served as the forty-second president of the United States from 1993 to 2001. Clinton became the second president to be impeached by the House of Representatives in 1998 following news of an affair with a White House intern. He is married to Hillary Rodham Clinton.

BOB BLAND (1982–): A white American fashion designer and activist. In 2017, Bland created and cochaired the 2017 Women's March alongside Carmen Perez, Linda Sarsour, and Tamika D. Mallory.

BOB MARLEY (1945–1981): A Jamaican singer, songwriter, and artist responsible for introducing international audiences to reggae music.

BUZZ ALDRIN (1930–): A white American engineer and former astronaut, who in 1969 became one of the first two humans to land on the moon.

CAROL BURNETT (1933–): A white American comedian and singer with a career spanning six decades in television. Her eponymous television program, *The Carol Burnett Show*, ran for eleven seasons from 1967 to 1978, paving the way for many women comedians in television.

CHIEN-SHIUNG WU (1912–1997): A Chinese American experimental physicist who became a key contributor to the World War II–era American research initiative known as the Manhattan Project. The Nobel Prize for her award-winning and eponymous Wu Experiment was given to her male colleagues Tsung-Dao Lee and Chen-Ning Yang in 1957 despite the fact *she* developed it.

CLARENCE THOMAS (1948–): A black American lawyer who has served as an associate justice of the Supreme Court of the United States since 1991. Thomas succeeded Thurgood Marshall and is the second African American to serve on the court.

DIANE NASH (1938–): A black American civil rights activist known for her role during the Civil Rights Movement. Nash is the cofounder of the Student Nonviolent Coordinating Committee and led non-violent direct-action efforts such as the Freedom Rides of 1961, during which she, John Lewis, and other student activists rode interstate buses into the segregated southern United States.

DONALD TRUMP (1946–): A white American businessperson and reality television personality who was elected the forty-fifth president of the United States. Using the campaign slogan, "Make America Great Again," Trump employed divisive, racist, intellectually dishonest rhetoric to win over white voters.

EDDIE HUANG (1982–): A Taiwanese American chef, author, entrepreneur, and attorney known for his memoir, *Fresh Off the Boat*, which chronicled his life as the son of Taiwanese immigrants, and was turned into an ABC sitcom.

EDWARD BULWER-LYTTON (1803–1873): An English author, poet, and playwright known for literary classics including *Devereaux* (1829), *Zanoni* (1842), and *The Last of the Barons* (1843). He penned such well-known phrases as "pursuit of the almighty dollar," "the pen is mightier than the sword," and "it was a dark and stormy night."

ERIC GARNER (1970–2014): A black American grandfather from Staten Island, New York, who was killed in an illegal chokehold in 2014 by NYPD Officer Daniel Pantaleo. His death and dying words, "I can't breathe," sparked protests of police violence across the country under the call to action #blacklivesmatter.

FANNIE LOU HAMER (1917–1977): A black American civil rights activist, community advocate, and voting rights organizer from Montgomery County, Mississippi. She was also a key organizer of the 1964 Mississippi Freedom Summer and worked alongside the Student Nonviolent Coordinating Committee.

FRANKLIN DELANO ROOSEVELT (1882–1945): A Dutch American politician, also known as FDR, who served as the thirty-second president of the United States from 1933 until his death in 1945. FDR was the longest-serving president of the United States. FDR also enacted the forced internment of immigrants and Americans of Japanese heritage in concentration camps during World War II.

GABBY DOUGLAS (1995–): A black American gymnast. She won gold medals in both the team and individual all-around competitions at the 2012 London Olympics, and a team gold medal at the 2016 Rio Olympics. She is the first woman of color of any nationality and the first African American gymnast in Olympic history to become the individual all-around champion.

GIL-SCOTT HERON (1949–2011): A black American soul and jazz poet, musician, and artist known for his advocacy that focuses style of spoken word poetry throughout the 1970s and 1980s.

DISABILITY RIGHTS ARE HUMAN RIGHTS

HARRY BELAFONTE (1927–): An American singer, actor, and activist of Jamaican and Martiniquan descent. Belafonte is known for his successful musical career which began in 1949, and for his early and continued support of the Civil Rights Movements of the past and present.

HILLARY RODHAM CLINTON (1947–): A white American politician who is married to Bill Clinton and was the first lady of the United States from 1993 to 2001. She also served as a senator from New York from 2001 to 2009, and the sixty-seventh secretary of state from 2009 to 2013.

IMANI BARBARIN (1990–): A black American woman with cerebral palsy who uses her social media platform and personal blog, *Crutches and Spice*, to discuss the intersecting experiences of blackness, disability, and womanhood.

JADA PINKETT SMITH (1971–): A black American actor and businessperson. As an activist, she hosted the 1997 Million Woman March in Philadelphia, and

as a philanthropist she has donated $1 million to the Baltimore School for the Arts in memory of her friend, Tupac Shakur.

JAMES BALDWIN (1924–1987): A black American writer, advocate, and social critic known for his activism in LGBTQ and black liberation. Baldwin's work includes *Giovanni's Room* (1956), *The Fire Next Time* (1963), *No Name in the Street* (1972), and many more.

JANET JACKSON (1966–): A black American award-winning singer, songwriter, dancer, and actor known for her socially conscious and provocative performances. Her musical career began in 1973, inspired by her older brothers' musical career in the critically acclaimed Jackson 5.

JAY-Z (1969–): A black American rapper, businessperson, and producer from Brooklyn, New York. Jay-Z is known for award-winning music business ventures such as the Roc-a-Fella music label, and marriage to cultural icon, Beyoncé Knowles-Carter.

JIMMY CARTER (1924–): A white American politician who served as the thirty-ninth president of the United States from 1977 to 1981.

JOE BIDEN (1942–): A white American politician who served as the forty-seventh vice president of the United States from 2009 to 2017. He also represented Delaware as a United States senator from 1973 to 2009.

JOHN LEWIS (1940–): A black American activist and congressman. In 1961, he volunteered to participate in the Freedom Rides, which challenged segregation at interstate bus terminals across the southern United States. From 1963 to 1966, Lewis was chairman of the

Student Nonviolent Coordinating Committee (SNCC). At the age of twenty-three, he was an architect of and a keynote speaker at the historic 1963 March on Washington for Jobs and Freedom. He has served as Representative of Georgia's Fifth District since 1987. He is the coauthor of the graphic novel trilogy, *March*, which is about the Freedom Rides and SNCC.

K.D. LANG (1961–): A white lesbian Canadian singer and songwriter known for her country-rock music and powerful vocals. She is an advocate of LGBTQ rights and animal rights.

KELLY ROWLAND (1981–): A black American singer, actor, and TV personality, who debuted her musical career alongside Beyoncé Knowles in Destiny's Child, one of the best-selling girl groups in history. As a solo artist, she has sold over forty million records. She is the author of *Whoa, Baby!: A Guide for New Moms Who Feel Overwhelmed and Freaked Out* (2017).

LANGSTON HUGHES (1902–1967): A black American author, activist, and poet who rose to prominence during the Harlem Renaissance in the 1920s. His work interrogates the duplicity of America's promises. Notable poems and essays by Hughes include "Let America Be America Again" (1935); "The Negro Artist and the Racial Mountain" (1926); "I, Too" (1926); and "Harlem" (1951).

LUCILLE BALL (1911–1989): A white American actor, comedian, and producer known for her eponymous shows, *I Love Lucy*, *The Lucy-Desi Comedy Hour*, *The Lucy Show*, *Here's Lucy*, and *Life with Lucy*. Her career spanned five decades from 1932 to 1986, paving the way for women in show business like Carol Burnett and countless others.

LUVVIE AJAYI (1985–): A Nigerian author, cultural critic, and writer. She is the author of the *New York Times* best selling book *I'm Judging You: The Do-Better Manual* (2016).

DR. MAE JEMISON (1956-): A black American engineer, physician, and NASA astronaut. She became the first African American woman to travel in space when she went into orbit aboard the space shuttle Endeavour on September 12, 1992.

MALCOLM X (1925–1965): A black American Muslim activist also known as el-Hajj Malik el-Shabazz. He was a faith leader, human rights activist, and cultural icon known for his advocacy of self-determination and self-defense against oppressive systems.

MARGARET CHO (1968–): A Korean American Grammy and Emmy Award nominated stand-up comedian, actor, and singer-songwriter.

DR. MARTIN LUTHER KING, JR. (1929–1968): A black American religious leader known for his role in advancing the Civil Rights Movement through the practice of nonviolent direct action. He fought for voting rights, LGBTQ equality, and against poverty, war, militarism, and racism.

MARS SEBASTIAN (1994–): A black American activist of Antiguan descent and cofounder of Black Out, an international movement to celebrate black joy and life in the face of anti-black oppression. In 2016 in response to the racism and sexism hurled at comedian Leslie Jones, Sebastian created the hashtag #LoveforLeslieJ as a call to action against hate.

MATTHEW SHEPARD (1976–1998): A white American student at the University of Wyoming, who on October 7, 1998, at the age of twenty-one, was brutally attacked, tied to a fence in a field outside of Laramie, and left to die in an anti-LGBTQ hate crime. On October 12, he died in a hospital in Fort Collins, Colorado. Today, his legacy lives on in the Matthew Shepard Foundation and in various films, plays, and other works of art.

MELISSA ETHERIDGE (1961–): A white lesbian American rock musician. Her 1988 self-titled debut album was certified double platinum. Following her public coming out in 1993, she has continued to be an outspoken advocate of LGBTQ equality.

MIA IVES-RUBLEE (1984–): A transracial Asian American adoptee with Osteogenesis Imperfecta who founded the Women's March Disability Caucus and uses social media to talk about racism, disability rights, adoption issues, immigration, and her dog.

MICHAEL BROWN (1996–2014): A black American high school graduate from Missouri who in 2014 was shot and killed by police officer Darren Wilson in an act of police violence. His death sparked protest across the country including months-long protests in Ferguson, Missouri, which defined a new era of grassroots action.

MICHELLE ROBINSON OBAMA (1964–): A black American lawyer and writer who was first lady of the United States from 2009 to 2017. She is married to the forty-fourth president of the United States, Barack Obama, and was the first African American first lady.

MYRA RICHARDSON (1999–): A black American activist from Baton Rouge, Louisiana, who in 2016 organized a youth-led Black Lives Matter rally on the steps of the Louisiana State Capitol in honor of Alton Sterling.

NEIL ARMSTRONG (1930–2012): A white American astronaut and aeronautical engineer who became the first person to walk on the moon in 1969.

PAUL ROBESON (1898–1976): A black American actor and singer during the Harlem Renaissance who became involved with the Civil Rights Movement. For his vocal stances on racial and political inequality, Robeson was criticized by government officials and labeled a communist.

RHEA BUTCHER (1982–): An LGBTQ rights activist and stand-up comedian from Akron, Ohio who is married to Cameron Esposito. Their first television series, *Take My Wife*, was hailed as a deeply necessary and authentic representation of LGBTQ relationships.

RONALD REAGAN (1911–2004): A white American Hollywood actor and politician who served as the fortieth president of the United States from 1981 to 1989. In 1982 he doubled down on an initiative started by President Nixon called "the war on drugs," which was responsible for increasing the number of people incarcerated for nonviolent drug law offenses from 50,000 in 1980 to more than 400,000 by 1997.

SANDRA BLAND (1987–2015): A twenty-eight-year-old black American found dead in her jail cell in Waller County, Texas, on July 13, 2015, three days after being arrested during a traffic stop. Her death sparked outrage across the country against police violence.

DR. TERRENCE ROBERTS (1941–): One of the Little Rock Nine, a group of African American students who, in 1957, were the first black students ever to attend classes at Little Rock Central High School in Little Rock, Arkansas. In 1999, he and the other people of the Little Rock Nine were awarded the Congressional Gold Medal by President Bill Clinton.

TIMBALAND (1972–): A black American rapper, producer, and songwriter who has worked with artists including Missy Elliott, Rihanna, and Jay-Z.

TINA KNOWLES (1954–): An American cultural icon and fashion designer of black and Creole heritage who is the mother of Beyoncé Knowles-Carter and Solange Knowles.

TRAYVON MARTIN (1995–2012): A seventeen-year-old black American high school student from Miami Gardens, Florida. In 2012, Trayvon was fatally shot in Sanford, Florida, by George Zimmerman, a neighborhood watch volunteer. In 2017, Florida University awarded a posthumous degree to Trayvon. Today, his legacy lives on in the Trayvon Martin Foundation.

TYRA BANKS (1973–): A black American supermodel, businessperson, and television host. She was the first black woman to be featured on the covers of *GQ* and the *Sports Illustrated Swimsuit Issue*. In 2003, she created the television show *America's Next Top Model*, which ushered in a new generation of supermodels from a myriad of backgrounds.

VALERIE JARRETT (1956–): A black American lawyer, businessperson, and civic leader. She served as the Senior Advisor to the President of the United States and Assistant to the President for Public Engagement and Intergovernmental Affairs in the Obama administration.

VENUS WILLIAMS (1980–): A black American tennis player and the sister of Serena Williams. Along with her sister, Venus has redefined the sport of tennis with her prowess as an athlete.

WAJEHA AL-HUWAIDER (1962–): A Saudi activist, writer, and cofounder of the Association for the Protection and Defense of Women's Rights in Saudi Arabia.

GLOSSARY

ORGANIZATIONS

The following organizations named in this book are good places to start if you want to learn more and get involved with progressive causes.

ACT UP!
An international advocacy organization working to positively impact the lives of people with HIV/AIDS, founded in 1987. **actupny.org**

AMERICORPS
A national organization in the United States providing opportunities for employment and volunteerism for young people across America. AmeriCorps places thousands of young adults into intensive service positions where they learn valuable work skills, earn money for education, and develop an appreciation for citizenship. **nationalservice.gov**

ARAB AMERICAN ASSOCIATION OF NEW YORK
An organization dedicated to supporting and empowering the Arab immigrant and Arab American community by providing services to help them adjust to their new home and become active members of society in New York City. **arabamericanny.org**

ATHLETE ALLY
A nonprofit organization dedicated to ending homophobia and transphobia in sports and educating athletic communities to stand up against hate. **athleteally.org**

AUDRE LORDE PROJECT
A New York City center for lesbian, gay, bisexual, two spirit, trans, and gender-nonconforming people. **alp.org**

BARRIOS UNIDOS
A youth violence prevention organization dedicated to providing community-based alternatives to detention for young people and re-entry opportunities to formerly incarcerated individuals. **barriosunidos.net**

BASIC RIGHTS OREGON
Works to ensure that all lesbian, gay, bisexual, transgender, and queer Oregonians experience equality by building a broad and inclusive politically powerful movement, shifting public opinion, and achieving policy victories. **basicrights.org**

BLACK ALLIANCE FOR JUST IMMIGRATION
Educates and engages African American and black immigrant communities to organize and advocate for racial, social, and economic justice. **baji.org**

BLACK LIVES MATTER GLOBAL NETWORK

A chapter-based, member-led organization whose mission is to build local power and to intervene in violence inflicted on black communities by the state and vigilantes. **blacklivesmatter.com**

CAMPAIGN ZERO

A data-informed platform building comprehensive solutions to end police violence in America, developed with contributions from activists, protesters, and researchers across the United States. **joincampaignzero.org**

CLARA LIONEL FOUNDATION

Supports and funds groundbreaking and effective education, health, and emergency response programs around the world. Founded in 2012 by Rihanna in honor of her grandparents, Clara and Lionel Braithwaite. **claralionelfoundation.org**

DIGNITY & POWER NOW

Founded by Patrisse Cullors, Dignity & Power Now is a grassroots organization based in Los Angeles, California, that fights for the dignity and power of incarcerated people, their families, and communities. **dignityandpowernow.org**

EQUALITY FOR HER

Founded by Blair Imani in January 2014, Equality for HER provides free educational resources about issues affecting women and gender nonbinary individuals. **equalityforher.org**

FAMILIA: TRANS QUEER LIBERATION MOVEMENT

A national organization that addresses, organizes, educates, and advocates for the issues most important to our lesbian, gay, bisexual, transgender, and queer (LGBTQ) and Latinx communities. **familiatqlm.org**

FERGUSON RESPONSE NETWORK

Ferguson Response Network was created to support nationwide efforts to support the important racial justice movement started in Ferguson, Missouri. **fergusonresponse.org**

THE GATHERING FOR JUSTICE

Founded in 2005 by Harry Belafonte to build a movement to end child incarceration while working to eliminate the racial inequities in the criminal justice system that perpetuate mass incarceration. **gatheringforjustice.org**

GLAAD

Focused on ending LGBTQ discrimination through media, GLAAD was founded in 1985 with the mission of promoting understanding, increasing acceptance, and advancing equality. **glaad.org**

HUMAN RIGHTS CAMPAIGN

The largest LGBTQ civil rights advocacy group and political lobbying organization in the United States. **hrc.org**

JUSTICE LEAGUE NYC

Brings diverse groups of young criminal justice experts, direct service providers, activists, advocates, artists, and formerly incarcerated individuals together to create a blueprint for reform in the criminal and social justice system in New York City and state. Cofounded by Carmen Perez and Marvin Bing, Jr., in 2013 as a task force of The Gathering for Justice. **gatheringforjustice.org/justiceleaguenyc**

MATTHEW SHEPARD FOUNDATION
An organization that teaches parents with children who may be questioning their sexuality to love and accept them for who they are, and to not throw them away. **matthewshepard.org**

MIRY'S LIST
Provides a mechanism for people to directly help new arrival refugee families with the things that they need to get started in their new lives in the United States, from diapers and beds to cleaning supplies and toiletries. **miryslist.org**

MOVEMENT FOR BLACK LIVES
A collective of more than fifty organizations representing thousands of black people from across the United States coming together to articulate a common vision and agenda for black liberation. **policy.m4bl.org**

MPOWER CHANGE
A grassroots movement rooted in diverse Muslim communities throughout the United States who are working together to build social, spiritual, racial, and economic justice for all people. **mpowerchange.org**

MUSLIM GIRL
Founded by Amani Al-Khatahtbeh in 2009, *Muslim Girl* is the leading online publication for Muslim women and provides a mainstream outlet through which Muslim women can define their own experiences. **muslimgirl.com**

NAACP
Founded February 12, 1909, the National Association for the Advancement of Colored People is the nation's oldest, largest, and most widely recognized grassroots-based civil rights organization. **naacp.org**

NATIONAL ACTION NETWORK (NAN)
Founded in 1991 by Reverend Al Sharpton, NAN works to promote a modern civil rights agenda that includes all people regardless of race, religion, ethnicity, citizenship, criminal record, economic status, gender, gender expression, or sexuality. **nationalactionnetwork.net**

NATIONAL DOMESTIC WORKERS ALLIANCE
America's leading voice for dignity and fairness for the millions of domestic workers in the United States, most of whom are women. **domesticworkers.org**

NATIVE APPROPRIATIONS
A forum for discussing representations of Native peoples, including stereotypes, cultural appropriation, news, activism, and more. Founded by Dr. Adrienne Keene in 2010. **nativeappropriations.com**

PLANNED PARENTHOOD
A trusted reproductive health care provider, an informed educator, a passionate advocate, and a global partner helping similar organizations around the world. **plannedparenthood.org**

SAPELO SQUARE

Sapelo Square is named for an island off the coast of Georgia which housed one of the first communities of African Muslims in the United States in the early 1800s. It is the first website dedicated to the comprehensive documentation and analysis of the black American Muslim experience. **sapelosquare.com**

SMITHSONIAN'S NATIONAL MUSEUM OF AFRICAN AMERICAN HISTORY AND CULTURE

Known also as the NMAAHC or Blacksonian, it is the only national museum devoted exclusively to the documentation of African American life, history, and culture. It was established by an act of Congress in 2003, following decades of efforts to promote and highlight the contributions of African Americans. **nmaahc.si.edu**

SOLUTIONS NOT PUNISHMENTS COALITION

A black, trans-led, broad-based collaborative working for a new Atlanta where every person has the opportunity to grow and thrive without facing unfair barriers, especially from the criminal justice system. **snap4freedom.org**

STAY WOKE

A nonprofit organization and digital accelerator that engages thousands of learners, builders, and activists in the work of advancing equity and justice in America. **staywoke.org**

TEACH FOR AMERICA

A diverse network of leaders who confront educational inequity through teaching and work with unwavering commitment from every sector of society to create a nation free from injustice. **teachforamerica.org**

TEGAN AND SARA FOUNDATION

An organization founded by Tegan and Sara Quin, which utilizes their platform to raise awareness and funds for LGBTQ issues and organizations across the United States and Canada. **teganandsarafoundation.org**

TRANSGENDER LAW CENTER

The largest American transgender-led civil rights organization in the United States, founded in 2002. **transgenderlawcenter.org**

TRANSKIDS PURPLE RAINBOW FOUNDATION

A foundation committed to enhancing the future lives of trans children and youth by educating schools, peers, places of worship, the medical community, government bodies, and society in general, in an effort to seek fair and equal treatment for all trans children and youth. **transkidspurplerainbow.org**

TRAYVON MARTIN FOUNDATION

A social justice organization committed to ending gun violence, strengthening families, and supporting women and girls. **trayvonmartinfoundation.org**

WOMEN'S MARCH

A women-led movement providing intersectional education on a diverse range of issues and creating entry points for new grassroots activists and organizers to engage in their local communities through trainings, outreach programs, and events. **womensmarch.com**

GLOSSARY

HASHTAGS

A hashtag is a pound or hash symbol (#) followed by a word or phrase used on social media to centralize conversations. In digital activism, hashtags often serve as calls to action. The following are some notable hashtags that have been created by the figures in this book.

#1000BLACKGIRLBOOKS: A campaign to crowdsource books with black girls as main characters and get them into the libraries of young readers. Created by Marley Dias.

#BLACKLIVESMATTER: A global movement was started by the hashtag #BlackLivesMatter in response the acquittal of George Zimmerman in the 2012 shooting of unarmed black teenager Trayvon Martin. Created by Alicia Garza, Patrisse Cullors, and Opal Tometi.

#DISABILITYTOOWHITE: Sheds light on the lack of diverse representation within the disability rights community. Created by Vilissa Thompson.

#DISABLEDANDCUTE: Started in February 2017, this hashtag showcases disabled people celebrating themselves and their bodies in an often-inaccessible world. Created by Keah Brown.

#GIRLSLIKEUS: Started in 2012, this hashtag has become a tool for all trans women to share and amplify each other's stories. Created by Janet Mock.

#GRABYOURWALLET: Following the 2016 release of vulgar statements made by presidential candidate Donald Trump in 2005, #GrabYourWallet became a movement to boycott unscrupulous retailers and seize on the political influence of women's consumer power. Created by Shannon Coulter and Sue Atencio.

#LOVE4GABBYUSA: Started in August 2016, this hashtag served as a call to action to support Olympic athlete Gabby Douglas following a slew of racist and sexist online harassment. Created by Leslie Jones.

#LOVEFORLESLIEJ: Started in July 2016, this hashtag served as a call to action to support comedian Leslie Jones following a slew of racist and sexist online harassment. Created by Mars Sebastian.

#TRANSBOOKDRIVE: Started in 2013 as an annual campaign to center the stories of transgender people and donate resources to members of the trans community. Created by Janet Mock.

#YOUOKSIS: Began in 2014 as an anti-harassment campaign to shed light on the sexual, physical, and verbal violence black women experience in the forms of street harassment, online harassment, and domestic abuse; creates a space for community dialogue. Created by Feminista Jones.

BLAIR IMANI

bl-AIR ee-MAH-nee

Blair Imani was born Blair Elizabeth Brown on October 31, 1993, in Los Angeles, California. Blair's dynamic family encouraged her passion for advocacy starting at a young age. As the only black child in her elementary school classes, Blair began to learn about discrimination and prejudice firsthand. In middle school, she became fascinated with the story of her neighbor Dr. Terrence Roberts and his role in integrating schools as one of the Little Rock Nine when he was fifteen. After conducting an interview with Dr. Roberts at the age of twelve, Blair started to understand that she too could make a difference.

At eighteen, Blair left California to begin her studies at Louisiana State University. Blair's activism began with her work on issues of LGBTQ inequality. Taking cues from organizers throughout history, Blair began teaching organizing tactics in the local community. As cases of police violence against unarmed black individuals proliferated across the country, Blair took to social media to maximize her impact as an organizer. In 2013, Blair began to organize mobilizations on Louisiana State University's campus.

In 2014, Blair founded Equality for HER, an education resource platform for women and nonbinary people. Through the organization, Blair developed a global network of coalition partners in Nigeria, Pakistan, Australia, Egypt, and in the United States. Working with activists in Muslim-majority countries introduced Blair to the Islamic faith. In 2015, she converted to Islam and changed her name to Blair Imani just prior to graduating from LSU.

To bring attention to the 2016 killing of Alton Sterling by police in Baton Rouge, Blair returned to her college town to support youth activist Myra Richardson as she organized a youth-led march to the Louisiana State Capitol Building. After the march concluded, Blair and community members continued to speak against police violence and the killing of Alton Sterling. That evening, marchers and protesters were confronted by special forces officers and Blair was dragged from where she stood by police, arrested, and held in East Baton Rouge Parish Prison.

Following this pivotal moment, Blair came to be seen as an activist in the public eye and used her new platform to speak out against hate and injustice. In the summer of 2017, she came out as a queer Muslim woman on national television and now works with GLAAD to use her visibility to silence stereotypes. Today, Blair is an author and activist. Find her on social media @blairimani and online at blairimani.com.

MONIQUE LE

mo-NEEK LAY

Monique Le was born on November 12, 1997, in Fairfax, Virginia, to two Vietnamese immigrant parents. Growing up, Monique did not appreciate her Vietnamese heritage as she would later in her life. As a child trying to assimilate to American life, she struggled to understand the way her grandfather and parents worked to preserve the cultural traditions of her heritage. For example, during lunchtime at school, she yearned for the staples of American food instead of the homemade Vietnamese cuisine her parents packed for her.

Art has been a significant part of Monique's life for as long as she can remember, and in elementary school, she first realized that art can uphold stereotypes around race. One day, Monique asked her classmate to pass her a crayon so she could draw her African American friend. In response, her classmate passed her the crayon named "black." Monique became deeply frustrated—there were so many shades of brown in the crayon box, yet her classmate opted for black. Monique grabbed the color she needed and continued coloring, but this was the first time she saw how, even in elementary school, color can perpetuate racial constructs. While Monique saw a beautiful cornucopia of diversity made of peach, apricot, and sepia tones, her classmates only saw yellow, red, and black. Monique believes that every culture and background has people from the entire spectrum of hues, and when we lump individuals into one bucket we fail to see the beauty within ourselves.

Monique spends her free time as a dental assistant for Hope for Tomorrow, a nonprofit health organization with the sole purpose of providing health and dental care to underprivileged communities in the United States, as well as the more rural areas of Vietnam where health care is less accessible. This work is the inspiration for her ambition to a career in the dental field.

Currently, Monique is a student and working as an illustrator. Just as she did as a child, she employs hundreds of shades, hues, and tones to bring leaders in human rights to life in her art.

ACKNOWLEDGMENTS

I wouldn't have been able to do the work of researching and writing this book without the support of so many people around me.

To start, I want to thank my many accomplices, for always being there for my many brainstorming sessions, for working one-on-one, and for believing in the project as much as they believed in me:

Monique Le, the amazing illustrator who worked tirelessly on weekends, between classes, and during exam periods to bring these stories to life with her vibrant illustrations. Monique and I first met on Twitter when I was scouting artists for Equality for HER's women's history month program. Within a few months of connecting online we had embarked on the journey that brought this book into your hands. Akeem Muhammad, for helping me stay determined throughout the entire process of creating this book and in my life. Akeem endured hours of excerpt readings as the book transformed into what it is today. Lori Rodriguez, for believing that we could make this book happen before I even believed it myself. Lori came up with the chapter titles and was always there with words of encouragement if I ever got bogged down or overwhelmed (which was often). Glendon Francis, for ensuring that this book got written. Without Glendon, I would still be procrastinating on Twitter or looking for individuals to feature in this text. In middle school, my best friend Bree Wernicke and I would spend recess and weekends making up languages, writing short stories, and enhancing our vocabularies. Bree believed in my ability as an author well before I did, and I am grateful for her constant support. My agent, Greta Moran, for using her genius in the world of publishing to get our book proposal into the hands of every editor and publishing house that would give us the time of day. Thanks to Greta, I had the fortuitous meeting in San Francisco with Ten Speed Press that brought this book to life.

Kaitlin Ketchum, the editor of *Modern HERstory* and an amazing movement ally, fought valiantly for the mission and message of this book to exist within the predominantly white world of publishing. Thanks to Kaitlin, I was pushed to add more depth and context to this book, enriching the lessons that it provides. Thanks also to Emma Campion, Mari Gill, Anne Goldberg, Serena Sigona, Natalie Mulford, Daniel Wikey, and Windy Dorresteyn at Ten Speed Press for all of their hard work on this book.

I am abundantly grateful for the support of LeVar Burton. Without LeVar's tireless advocacy of youth literacy and initiatives like *Reading Rainbow*, I would not even be able to read. On August 3, 2017, LeVar retweeted one of my posts about *Modern HERstory* to his two million Twitter followers with the call to action: "Somebody publish this woman's book!"

Instantly publishers were eager to read my proposal for *Modern HERstory*, and this momentum paved the way getting my book into your hands.

I am grateful for the wisdom of my mentors, including Taye Hansberry, Feminista Jones, and Brittany Packnett. When I expressed interest in the world of beauty and fashion, Taye brought me on as an intern and taught me everything I know about digital media communications. When I told Feminista that a publisher wanted to see my book proposal—and that I had no clue how to make one—she stopped everything, called me from her office, and told me how to put a book proposal together. Brittany is the personification of generosity—she has helped me through so much and has opened the door to opportunities I would otherwise never have imagined possible.

Thanks also to Katelyn Burns, Ren Drincic, Fadumo Osman, Fajr DeLane, Dierra Bynum-Reid Shay-Akil McLean, Clarkisha Kent, Anisa Yudawanti, Brittany Witter, and Mariel Limon for helping make *Modern HERstory* as inclusive as possible.

I am also grateful to my mentors Andrew Walker, Marcus Mason, Andrew Aydin, Dr. Stephen Finley, Van Jones, Bob and Roberta Smith, Dr. Lori Martin, Johua DuBois, DeRay Mckesson, Dawn Laguens, and Sarah Kate Ellis for believing in me throughout my career and for inspiring me to push harder and reach higher.

I am grateful to all of my many, *many* cousins, and my elders Uncle Craig and Auntie Cyndee, Big Gregory, Little Gregory, Uncle Vernon, Auntie Cynthia, Auntie Marsha, Auntie Karen and Uncle Roby, Uncle Steve and Auntie Debbie, Uncle Terry and Auntie Rita, and Grandpa Nolan.

I am especially grateful for my grandmothers Grandma Eloise, Grandma Marlene, and Grandma Verna Jean. Each of my grandmothers have made history in their lifetimes and helped me be the fiery and confident black woman that I am today.

I want to thank my mother and father for always being ready to enter into a new chapter of my life, no matter what. You raised me to be an understanding and compassionate person, and my upbringing is at the heart of my advocacy today. I know that I often terrify the both of you (especially the first time I got arrested at a protest), but I want to thank you for always jumping into action and getting in the trenches with me. You are the best parents anyone could ask for.

Finally, I appreciate my siblings no end. Nancy, Marlena, Brandon, and Chelsea have each taught me lessons about life for which I am endlessly grateful. I know I am often ridiculous and way too political, but I couldn't have written this book without each of you in my life.

INDEX

A

Aaliyah, 74, 173
ACT UP!, 6, 180
Aditi Juneja, 87
Adrienne Keene, 113, 182
African American Policy Forum, 23
Alencia Johnson, 114, 122
Alice Walker, 168, 173
Alice Wong, 87, 173
Alicia Garza, 18–19, 24, 27, 28, 185
Alissa Lentz, 136
Allison Renville, 41
Al Sharpton, 35, 173, 182
Alton Sterling, 95, 173, 178
Amandla Stenberg, 88
Amani Al-Khatahtbeh, 133, 135
AmeriCorps, 58, 180
Angela Davis, 27, 173
Ani DiFranco, 151, 173
Anita Hill, 46, 173
Anjali Paray, 117
Anna Wintour, 174
A. Philip Randolph, 167
Arab American Association of New
    York, 32, 180
asha bandele, 27, 173
Association for the Protection and
    Defense of Women's Rights in
    Saudia Arabia, 179
Athlete Ally, 121, 180
Attallah Shabazz, 170

B

Audre Lorde, 27, 173
Audre Lorde Project, 151, 180
Ava DuVernay, 65, 162

Barack Hussein Obama, 35, 41,
    42, 70, 85, 114, 118, 155, 158,
    173–74, 178, 179
Barbara Walters, 157, 174
Barrios Unidos, 31, 180
Basic Rights Oregon, 122, 180
Bayard Rustin, 167
bell hooks, 27, 174
Bernice King, 20, 174
Bernie Sanders, 144, 174
Beyoncé Knowles-Carter, 81, 174,
    177, 179
Bill Clinton, 70, 77, 174, 176, 179
Black Alliance for Just
    Immigration, 28, 180
Black Lives Matter Global
    Network, 19, 28, 180
Black Lives Matter movement,
    18–19, 21, 24, 27, 28, 54, 81,
    144, 175, 178, 185
Black Lives of Unitarian
    Universalism, 143
Black Out, 178
Black Panther Party, 46, 126, 167
Black Twitter, 42, 91, 167
Blair Imani, 181

C

Bob Bland, 20, 31, 35, 174
Bobby Seale, 167
Bob Marley, 161, 174
Brittany Packnett, 42
Buzz Aldrin, 2, 174

Cameron Esposito, 66
Campaign Zero, 42, 181
Carlotta Walls LaNier, 170
Carmen Perez, 20, 31, 35, 174, 181
Carol Burnett, 73, 174, 177
Chen-Ning Yang, 174
Chien-Shiung Wu, 174
Civil Rights Act of 1964, 2, 169
Civil Rights Movement, 23, 168,
    172, 175, 176, 177, 178
Clara Braithwaite, 147, 181
Clara Lionel Foundation, 147, 181
Clarence Thomas, 46, 175
Constance Wu, 69
Coretta Scott King, 174
critical race theory, 23, 167
cultural appropriation, 88, 113,
    168, 182

D

Dakota Access Pipeline (DAPL), 41
Daniel Pantaleo, 31, 175
Darren Wilson, 178

Derald Sue, 170
Diane Nash, 23, 175
Dignity & Power Now, 27, 181
Disability Visibility Project, 173
Donald Trump, 19, 32, 87, 135, 148, 171, 175, 185
Dorothy Vaughan, 12, 14, 162
Dwight D. Eisenhower, 170

E

Eddie Huang, 69, 175
Eddie Murphy, 165
Edward Bulwer-Lytton, 38, 175
Elizabeth Eckford, 170
Ellen DeGeneres, 63, 70
Eman Idil Bare, 139
Eman Idil Designs, 139
Equality for HER, 122, 181
Eric Garner, 31, 175
Ernest Green, 170

F

Familia: Trans Queer Liberation Movement, 118, 181
Fannie Lou Hamer, 23, 175
Feminista Jones, 91, 167, 185
Fenty Beauty, 147
Ferguson Response Network, 143, 181
Flint water crisis, 158

Franchesca Ramsey, 92
Franklin Delano Roosevelt (FDR), 11, 175
Freedom Rides, 175, 176

G

Gabby Douglas, 73, 175, 185
The Gathering for Justice, 31, 181
Gay Activists Alliance, 6
Gay Liberation Front, 6
George Zimmerman, 18, 24, 179, 185
Geraldine Roman, 45
Gil-Scott Heron, 81, 175
GLAAD, 157, 181
Gloria Ray Karlmark, 170

H

Harlem Renaissance, 8, 169, 177, 178
Harry Belafonte, 31, 176, 181
hashtags, 185
HERO backpacks, 136
Hillary Rodham Clinton, 165, 176
Huey Newton, 167
Human Rights Campaign, 121, 181

I

Ibtihaj Muhammad, 140
Ilyasah Shabazz, 170

Imani Barbarin, 50, 176
intersectionality, 18–21, 23, 31, 121, 169–70
Issa Rae, 92, 95

J

Jackie Aina, 96
Jada Pinkett Smith, 73, 170, 176
James Baldwin, 8, 176
Jamilah Lemieux, 46
Janet Jackson, 49, 74, 176
Janet Mock, 6, 49, 99, 185
Jay-Z, 147, 176, 179
Jazz Jennings, 155, 157
Jefferson Thomas, 170
Jennicet Gutiérrez, 6, 118
Jimmy Carter, 11, 176
Joe Biden, 35, 176
John Lewis, 165, 175, 176–77
Justice League NYC, 32, 181

K

Kat Blaque, 99
Katherine Johnson, 12, 15, 162
Kazimierz Czarnecki, 14
k.d. lang, 151, 177
Keah Brown, 50, 185
Kelly Rowland, 81, 177
Kimberlé Crenshaw, 18, 168, 170, 171

The King Center, 174
Knowles, Solange, 81, 174, 179
Knowles, Tina, 81, 179

L

Langston Hughes, 8, 177
Layshia Clarendon, 121
Les Indivisibles, 54
Leslie Jones, 73, 178, 185
Leslie Mac, 132, 143, 144
LGBTQ Rights Movement, 5, 170
Linda Sarsour, 20, 31, 32, 35, 174
Lionel Braithwaite, 147, 181
Little Rock Nine, 170, 179
Lori Rodriguez, 122
Lorraine Hansberry, 8, 104
Lucille Ball, 73, 177
Luvvie Ajayi, 92, 177

M

Mae Jemison, 162, 177
Malcolm X, 126, 170, 177
Manal al-Sharif, 53
March for Equality and Against
    Racism (1983), 54, 167
March on Washington for Jobs and
    Freedom (1963), 20, 35, 167,
    177, 179
Margaret Cho, 73, 177
Margaret Thatcher, 174
Mari Copeny, 155, 158
Marissa Jenae Johnson, 132,
    143–44
Marley Dias, 155, 161, 185
Marsha P. Johnson, 5–6, 110, 172
Mars Sebastian, 73, 178, 185

Martin Luther King, Jr., 20, 65,
    167, 174, 177
Marvin Bing, Jr., 181
Mary Jackson, 12, 14, 162
Matthew Shepard, 70, 178
Matthew Shepard Foundation,
    178, 182
Maxine Waters, 170
Melba Pattillo Beals, 170
Melissa Etheridge, 151, 178
Mia Ives-Rublee, 50, 178
Michael Brown, 42, 54, 178
Michelle Phan, 100
Michelle Robinson Obama, 74,
    162, 178
Million Woman March (1997),
    170, 176
Minnijean Brown, 170
Miry's List, 69, 182
Missy Elliott, 62, 74, 103, 179
Mona Haydar, 103
Movement for Black Lives, 19,
    144, 182
MPower Change, 32, 182
Myra Richardson, 81, 178

N

NAACP (National Association for
    the Advancement of Colored
    People), 31, 88, 96, 165, 182
NASA, 12, 14–15, 162, 177
National Action Network (NAN),
    31, 35, 182
National Domestic Workers
    Alliance, 24, 182
National Museum for African

American History and Culture
    (NMAAHC), 28, 183
Native Appropriations, 182
Neil Armstrong, 2, 178

O

Obama Foundation, 174
Opal Tometi, 19, 24, 27, 28, 185
Oprah Winfrey, 49, 62, 63, 70, 77,
    162, 165

P

Patrisse Cullors, 18–19, 24, 27, 28,
    173, 181, 185
Patsy Takemoto Mink, 11
Paul Robeson, 8, 178
Peggy McIntosh, 171
Phile Chionesu, 170
Planned Parenthood, 69, 114,
    122, 182
POWER (People Organized to Win
    Employment Rights), 24

R

Ramp Your Voice!, 107
Raquel Willis, 6, 110, 125
The Resistance, 87, 148, 171
Rhea Butcher, 66, 179
Richard Nixon, 172, 179
Rihanna, 133, 147, 179, 181
Rokhaya Diallo, 54
Ronald Reagan, 31, 172, 179
Roxane Gay, 50, 57

S

Safety Pin Box, 132–33, 143, 144
Sandra Bland, 23, 171, 179
Sandy Ho, 58
Sapelo Square, 126, 182
Sara Quin, 151, 183
Say Her Name, 23, 171
Serena Williams, 78, 179
Serena Williams Foundation, 78
Shannon Coulter, 148, 185
Solutions Not Punishments
        Coalition, 125, 183
Standing Rock, 41
Stay Woke, 87, 183
Stonewall Riots, 5–6
Street Transvestite Action
        Revolutionaries (STAR), 6, 172
Student Nonviolent Coordinating
        Committee (SNCC), 46, 172,
        175, 176
Su'ad Abdul Khabeer, 126
Sue Atencio, 185
Sylvia Rivera, 5–6, 49, 110, 172

T

Tamika D. Mallory, 20, 31, 35, 174
Taye Hansberry, 104
Taylor Richardson, 162
Teach for America, 42, 183
Tegan and Sara Foundation,
        151, 183
Tegan Quin, 151, 183
Teresa Shook, 19–20
Terrence Roberts, 170, 179
Thelma Mothershed, 170
Thurgood Marshall, 175

Timbaland, 74, 179
Title IX, 11, 172
Transgender Law Center, 125, 183
TransKids Purple Rainbow
        Foundation, 157, 183
Trayvon Martin, 18, 24, 54, 179, 185
Trayvon Martin Foundation,
        179, 183
Tsung-Dao Lee, 174
Tupac Shakur, 176
Tyra Banks, 129, 179

V

Valerie Jarrett, 35, 179
Vanessa Wruble, 20
Venus Williams, 78, 179
Vilissa Thompson, 107, 185

W

Wajeha al-Huwaider, 53, 179
War on Drugs, 31, 172, 179
Williams Sister Fund, 78
Winnie Harlow, 129
Winnie Madikizela-Mandela, 170
Women's March, 20–21, 31, 32,
        35, 49, 110, 125, 174, 178, 183

Y

Yara Shahidi, 165

Ten Speed Press and the Ten Speed Press colophon are registered
trademarks of Penguin Random House LLC.

Library of Congress Cataloging-in-Publication Data
Names: Imani, Blair, author.
Title: Modern HERstory : stories of women and nonbinary people rewriting history /
Blair Imani; foreword by Tegan and Sara ; illustrated by Monique Le.
Other titles: Modern her story
Description: California: Ten Speed Press, 2018. | Includes
bibliographical references and index.
Identifiers: LCCN 2018009380
Subjects: LCSH: Women political activists—United States—Biography. |
Leadership in women—United States. | Social movements—United States. |
Social change—United States. | BISAC: BIOGRAPHY & AUTOBIOGRAPHY / Women. |
SOCIAL SCIENCE / Women's Studies. | POLITICAL SCIENCE /
Political Process / Political Advocacy.
Classification: LCC HQ1236.5.U6 I523 2018 | DDC 320.082/0973—dc23
LC record available at https://lccn.loc.gov/2018009380

Hardcover ISBN: 978-0-399-58223-3
eBook ISBN: 978-0-399-58224-0

Printed in China

Design by Emma Campion
Illustrations by Monique Le

10 9 8 7 6 5 4 3

"Blair Imani's *Modern HERstory* is like a woman's heart. Filled with compassion, understanding, and acceptance, the book embraces women of diverse experiences, including transwomen like myself, in order to inspire people to aspire and work for a happier and more inclusive society for all. When you feel like giving up, you have got to read this book!"

—Representative Geraldine Roman, first openly transgender member of the Philippines Congress

———————

"With *Modern HERstory*, Blair Imani provides readers with crucial insight to understanding modern social justice movements in a way that is both vital and accessible. By shining a light on contemporary women and nonbinary people who are making history in real time, some lesser known than others, Imani reminds readers that heroes can emerge from anywhere, that activism takes many shapes and forms, and that history is not simply a matter of the past but something occurring in real time and in powerfully unexpected ways. The people presented here do not represent a new type of activism; rather, they represent people who've long been present in freedom movements and are too often overlooked."

—Bree Newsome, artist and activist